QUESTIONS YOU'VE ASKED ABOUT SEXUALITY

ALBERTA MAZAT

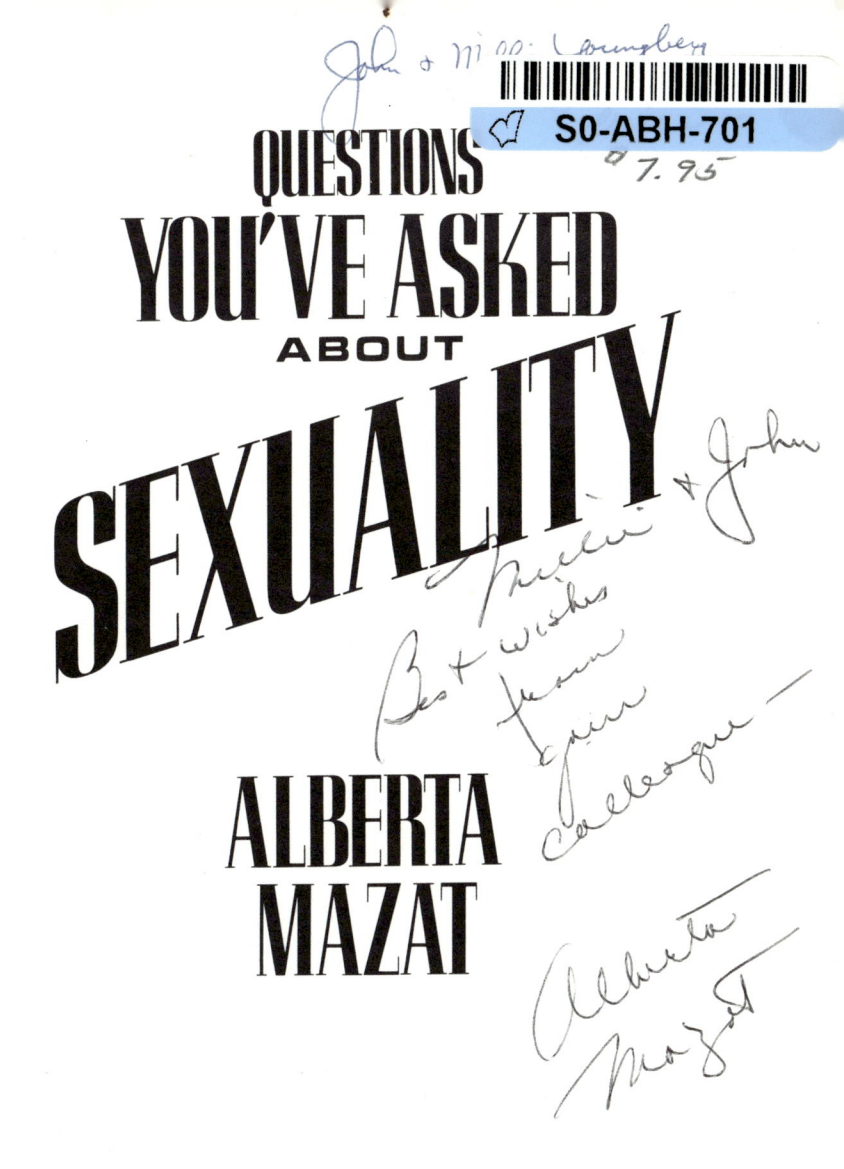

Pacific Press Publishing Association
Boise, Idaho
Oshawa, Ontario, Canada

Edited by Glen Robinson
Designed by Tim Larson
Typeset in 10/12 Bookman

Copyright © 1991 by
Pacific Press Publishing Association
Printed in the United States of America
All Rights Reserved

Library of Congress Cataloging in Publication Data:
Mazat, Alberta, 1919-
  Questions you've asked about sexuality/Alberta Mazat.
      p.   cm.
    ISBN 0-8163-1038-6
    1. Sex instruction—Miscellanea. 2. Sex instruction—Religious aspects—Christianity—Miscellanea. 3. Sex customs—Miscellanea. 4. Sexual ethics—Miscellanea.   I. Title.
HQ21.M4618   1991
306.7'07—dc20   90-21378
                                                           CIP

91 92 93 94 95 ● 5 4 3 2 1

Contents

To Begin With 5

But First 7

Chapter 1:
Infants and Children Are Sexual Too 9

Chapter 2:
Teens Have Questions About the "S" Word 32

Chapter 3:
Unmarried Adults Are Asking 57

Chapter 4:
Beyond the "I Do's" 74

Chapter 5:
The Anniversaries Go By 102

Chapter 6:
No Retirement Age for Sexuality 116

The Conclusion of the Whole Matter 126

To begin with . . .

Let me tell you how this book came to be written. Actually, you were, in part, responsible! You see, for some twenty years I have been talking with people in churches, schools, conventions, and community groups about sexuality. I have interacted with many of you in seminars, workshops, club meetings, Bible Camps, weeks of devotion, encampments, and retreats. Your interest in the material presented was always rewarding. But what I found most challenging, and you seemed to find most helpful, was dedicating time to answering your questions.

Because the subject of sexuality is more sensitive than many other topics, I found that having you write out your questions, rather than asking them out loud, gave you a greater sense of freedom to ask. The questions were anonymously presented, and covered many aspects of sexuality.

After each trip, I popped these little stacks of questions into a special box marked with a big question mark (?). I soon realized that many people out there were asking the same questions! Many stated that they had no one to go to with their concerns. I decided to sort out all these papers and look them over with the idea of seeing what I could come up with.

That was a most interesting experience! The questions came from persons of all age groups, from junior teens to older retirees. They were written on a variety of materials in a rainbow of colors. Some were penned on lovely sheets of notepaper provided by an artistic coordinator and beautifully decorated with a floral design. Some were simply on utilitarian note sheets. Others were on torn bits of notebook paper (these most frequently from school groups). Backs of bank receipt slips, paper towels, and church bulletins sometimes served as paper. Pages torn from diaries were there. Some were in languages foreign to me and carefully translated so that I could respond to them. (Then, of course, the answers were translated back into the questioner's language.) Some used handouts that I had provided for earlier meetings, which was somewhat disquieting! However, it demonstrated that what people want to know because of their own experience was more important to them than a speaker's agenda.

Some questions were asked over and over again, from many different ages and many different geographical areas. From all this, I conceived the idea of providing a forum for the discussion of the questions most frequently asked. A book became that medium. Here it is in your hands!

As I wrote it, my eyes may have been on my typewriter, but my mind kept picturing groups of you here and there: College Heights, Canada; Zillah, Washington; Honolulu, Hawaii; Brisbane, Australia; Bakersfield, California; Tampere, Finland, and many other wonderful places. I am going to talk to you in this book as though we were all together again, for all of you have been the inspiration for putting into writing some of the discussions we have had on questions dealing with sexuality.

None of the questions have been "planted" by me. All are copied as you wrote them. Occasionally your note has been edited to a shorter version of the original, but the words remain unaltered.

But first . . .

Let me show you one of the most reasonable and important questions I was ever asked. This was at a gathering of academy students. Here it is:

How do we know that you know what you are talking about? How do we know that you know the right things to do, or why should we listen to you? What qualifications or experience have you had?

I like that question. It demonstrated good thinking on the part of that young writer. Surely you have a right to know what preparation entitles me to take on this responsibility. So here it is: my undergraduate degree from the University of Denver was in sociology; a Masters degree from the same institution was in social work, with emphasis on marriage and family therapy.

On my office walls are pieces of paper affirming that I am a Licensed Marriage and Family Therapist, and a Licensed Clinical Social Worker in the State of California. The American Association for Sex Educators, Counselors, and Therapists has certified me individually as each of these; and the American Association for Marriage and Family Therapy registers me as a clinical member. The National Council for Family Relations certifies me as a Family Life Educator.

For many years Loma Linda University, in Loma Linda, California, elected me a professor of marriage and family, where human sexuality was one of my areas of assignment. During this time I was also involved in providing therapy for individuals and marriages in the area of sexuality, along with other problem spots.

Not the least of my valuable experience has been as the wife of an exceptionally loving and supportive husband, and the mother of four wonderful adult children, who have taught me more than I taught them. Add for good measure five entirely special grandchildren who keep me current on life!

However, I certainly do not wish to pose as someone who has all the answers. I do not. I would rather be thought of as a fellow traveler who has tried to find out as much as possible about our response to the gift of sexuality. My dearest wish is that coming together in this book, we may learn better how to demonstrate that God's plan for the sexuality of His children is a good and gracious one.

The questions are divided into concerns involving infants and children, those of teens and young adults (married and single), and those married for longer periods of time. I cannot begin to answer every question I have received, but I have tried to include those most frequently asked and the ones which stirred up the most interest in the answering.

So let's get on with the questions!

Chapter 1

Infants and Children Are Sexual Too

Sometimes we feel that infants and children aren't really sexual, that they are just neutral little beings until they are hormonally "awakened" later in their lives. This is not true, however. Remember the first thing you wanted to know about your new baby—"Is it a girl or a boy?" We begin to identify the baby in our minds as female or male, and then we begin to make differences in the way we relate to them.

Studies done in hospitals indicate that little girls are cooed to, cuddled, and spoken to more frequently—and in a higher-pitched voice—than little boys are. Little boys are held differently, spoken to in a deeper, louder voice, and proudly credited with being big, noisy, and active—which seems to be desirable for little boys. We are more likely to say about a little girl, "Isn't she adorable?" and to a little boy, "Isn't he a bruiser?"

Parents have a wonderful opportunity early in their care of their babies to include a good feeling about their bodies. By patting, stroking, and caressing, they demonstrate not only their loving concern, but the realization that their little ones can experience good body feelings. Meeting needs in a consistent, tender way teaches trust. Using loving tones and smiling chatter demonstrates the joys of communication. Each of these early experiences—touching, experiencing, trusting, and communicating—can be part of the preparation for good sexuality later in life.

Now for some of the questions parents have asked most frequently about their little ones.

Sex Education in the Home

At what age should you start to tell your children about sex?

If you are talking about sexuality in general, you can see from the above response that we begin teaching as soon as we bring babies home from their birthing place. But this question probably means, When do we start to tell about "the facts of life"? I have to tell you, my answer would still be the same: as soon as you bring the baby home. "Now, really," you are probably thinking, "that is a bit much! A small baby can't understand what you are talking about." Precisely! That is why I suggest this time frame. You see, for several years now you can begin to get your act together. I have discovered that telling about the beginning of life is one of the most difficult tasks for parents. We delay, fumble, and try to give away the responsibility to the other parent or anyone willing to take it.

I remember once being told by the leaders, before I talked to a group of preteens, that parents had come to them in advance, requesting, "Tell Alberta to talk to them about *everything!* We have never talked to them about sex. We don't know what to say."

If you start telling your tiny infant, you can prepare yourself to be more comfortable and effective later. You can begin talking out loud about vaginas and penises, about eggs and sperms, about intercourse and conception—the works! He or she will simply coo and smile back without the faintest idea of what marvelous news is being imparted. Being talked to gently is always a good experience for a baby. This way you can begin to become comfortable with the words and the message. When you repeat it often enough, in different forms and versions, you can perfect it until it sounds just right to you. Then when your child is ready to hear the good news, you will be full of poise and come off sounding like a pro!

Do you think sex education in the family should be prescheduled for a certain time, or only as the children ask?

Probably both. But if you wait for some children to ask, they may be ready to leave for college first! Sometimes the reason for this is that your child may not be a very communicative one, and does very little asking about anything. Other times it is possible that the child has received cues,

INFANTS AND CHILDREN ARE SEXUAL TOO

intentionally or unintentionally given, that things get a little tense when sex is mentioned. One child voiced it this way: "In our house we don't talk about those things; it makes everyone nervous." You can be absolutely certain of one thing: they *do* have questions, and they *do* want to know.

Learning about sex should be a gradual unfolding, not a one-time shot like an inoculation. As we speak freely about parts of the body (calling them by their correct names), and as we explain the beauty and development of our wonderfully created bodies, including the genital parts, we make it easier for children to ask questions. Nothing is more important in sex education than being "askable" so that our children know there is one sure source of correct information.

Which parent should tell the child, whether boy or girl?

Both parents should be involved in talking with both daughters and sons. Sometimes parents can talk to them together, another time Mom and Dad can talk to Hortense or Hector individually. (Hortense and Hector will be used throughout this book as our generic names for boys and girls.) Studies have shown that sex education is done most often by mothers. Unfortunately, fathers usually give over this responsibility. Since both parents are usually ill-prepared because of their own backgrounds, this indicates that mothers may be around their children more. But that is no reason for this pattern to continue.

Fathers need to be involved. They have so much to contribute. They can not only model, but explain to their sons the privilege of being male and the responsibilities that this brings. They can share their own childhood experiences and feelings. What times of closeness this will bring! Fathers can make their daughters feel special, can help them learn to value their bodies and make good decisions about their sexuality. They can teach them how to protect themselves from opportunists.

Mothers can explain experiences of womanhood to their daughters. They can identify with their daughters' feelings and answer more sensitively the sexual questions that their

12   QUESTIONS YOU'VE ASKED ABOUT SEXUALITY

daughters have. They can serve as a sounding board for their sons, helping them to see the female point of view and engendering respect for their bodies and those of the opposite sex. Can you envision what sort of young people would come out of homes which prepare them in this manner? Sex education like this is an ongoing process. It is picked up by one or the other parent regularly and at appropriate times. Sometimes the whole family unit can be involved in discussions and share an interest in current affairs. Discussions about teen pregnancy, AIDS, abortion, etc., can provide an entry into deeper, more personal talks. Adult material? Don't be deceived. Your grade-schoolers are already hearing about these things and deserve to be informed by loving parents with high moral values.

Do we need to provide visual aids in order to make the explanations clearer?

Often these can be very helpful. Many Christian bookstores supply excellent books with dignified text and pictures. After looking, you may decide that you prefer the line drawings to photographs. I know I do. Browse around some of these stores and pick the books that you feel you could be most comfortable sharing with your child. Don't just hand books to your children, even if Hortense and Hector can read. Use them as tools to make it easier to clarify your story.

Is there some deadline when children should know certain things about sex?

I believe that before Hector and Hortense enter school, they should have certain information. Hopefully this will have been given in small segments, well in advance—not on the day they are walking out the door to start kindergarten!

1. Children should know the correct anatomical names for body parts and body functions. From the very beginning, there should be no silly little euphemisms for this information. There are usually as many different names for genital parts as there are playmates. That is very confusing to our children, since other body parts have

names common to all. This needlessly mystifies a whole area of sexuality. What if they use these correct words in front of others? Good! Then more people can become educated. One grandmother told of her little granddaughter exclaiming after she got off an amusement ride that the dips and falls had tickled her right in the vagina! Nothing horrible happened at all; they were not thrown out of the park! She said that people were smiling delightedly. As children grow older, they learn the appropriateness of talking about their body needs and parts. Meanwhile, no harm will come from a few slips in front of nonfamily members, for which children should certainly not be shamed or punished.

2. Children should know that babies grow inside their mothers, but are a product of both Mommy and Daddy. This will have to be carefully explained. (See next question.)

3. Children should know that mommies can nourish their babies by breast-feeding, God's special way of taking extra good care of them. This will be the beginning of their realization that breasts are more than sex symbols.

4. Children need to understand that their bodies are gifts from God and that a special part of that body exists which is uniquely theirs. No one should be allowed to touch the genital parts of their bodies—not their new friends or schoolmates, not any of the school staff or anyone around the playground. They should be given instruction and permission to say a very loud "NO" and run to an adult in charge. They are to report what happened to them so that they can be protected. Hopefully you have already given your child permission to say this kind of a No to other family members as well, including those who live outside the home. Very rarely are small children molested by unknown people, by strangers. They are usually acquainted with the perpetrators. This is a hard thing to say, but our little ones *must be protected* from this kind of abuse. (More about this later.)

Could you give a demonstration on how parents can explain sex to a small child? The part about the baby.

This is usually the hardest part for parents. So let's go through this as though you were talking to Hector or Hortense some time after there seemed to be an interest, or you wondered why there wasn't! Pick a relaxed, unhurried time when the family is together in a pleasant setting.

"Isn't it great to have our family all together like this? [Gather in a loving embrace.] It's fun to hug like this, isn't it? Did you know that there are lots of different kinds of family hugs? There are Hortense and Daddy hugs, there are Hortense and Mommy hugs, there are Mommy and Daddy hugs, and there are Mommy, Daddy, and Hortense hugs—when we all hug at once, a great big family hug! [Each type of hug can be demonstrated.] Families hug each other to show their love, don't they?

"You know, before we had our little Hortense, there was only one kind of hug in our family, and that was a Mommy and Daddy hug. Mommy and Daddy loved each other so much that they would hug often, sometimes in the kitchen when they were doing the dishes or in the living room when they watched television. Sometimes they would hug each other when they went to bed. One time they got to thinking. 'We have so much love in this family, wouldn't it be great if we had another person to share this with? Maybe we should have a little Hortense so we could have one more hugger in the family.'

"The more they talked about it, the better the idea sounded. Then they planned for you with a very special kind of hug. You remember we have talked about the part of the body that makes a man a Daddy, the penis? And remember the part of the body that makes a woman a Mommy, a vagina? In this special Mommy-Daddy hug, Daddy put his Daddy-part, the penis, right inside the Mommy-part, the vagina. Then something very wonderful happened. Something came out of Daddy's penis, called semen. In this semen were many, many tiny little sperms, or seeds, that wanted to find their way to the egg in Mommy's body so a baby could begin to grow.

"You see, it takes both a daddy's sperm and a mommy's egg to get a baby started. So the sperms hurried on their way to try to find the egg through a narrow little tube called the Fallopian tube [with a younger child, this specific name is not necessary]. When the sperms found the egg, they all tried very hard to get through the covering of the egg in Mommy's body. Each of them wanted to be the one to start Hortense. But the strongest, most beautiful, and best one made its way through that covering, and joined the life that was waiting there to start Hortense. Now something very wonderful happened. So that no other sperms could get through, that egg covering suddenly became so tough that all the rest had to stay out! It was like putting up a big No Entrance sign, so that little Hortense would be the only one in that very special place.

"Now the tiny little bundle of Hortense had to find a place big enough to grow in. And God had that all ready. The name of the place is the uterus. It is such a special place in a Mommy's body that nothing else ever happens here except a baby growing. God knew just how to take the very best care of you in the very best place. This place was warm and soft, and had just the right food you needed to grow on. [*Please* avoid making this growth place the mommy's tummy. Many children have been turned off by this part of the story by having visions of being in an enclosure where peas and carrots occasionally rained down on their heads! That is messy! And it isn't special enough. God's plan is much more beautiful.]

"Now, Hortense, you grew and grew in that special place. Pretty soon we could see that Mommy's tummy was getting larger. Then one day Mommy felt your little leg kick, and how excited we were, for we knew then that you were very real. We used to like to feel and watch you kick. We would wonder what you were going to look like, how much you would weigh, how big you would be. We spent a lot of time thinking about what we would name you and how careful we would be to try to take good care of you.

"Then one day you must have thought, 'I've been in here long enough! It's getting crowded because I have grown so much. Besides, I want to see this Mommy and this Daddy who talk to me so gently and pat me so lovingly. I want out!'

"Mommy felt your 'knock,' and she and Daddy knew that it was time to go to the place where they take special care of babies that come out of the Mommy-homes. Finally you came out through the special place where the sperms first went into the vagina. The opening stretched and stretched until your little head poked out, and you started to cry. How thrilled we were to hear your voice for the first time.

"They let us hold you and talk to you for a long time. We knew you could tell we were your parents and that we loved you. We looked over your tiny little hands, your feet, your whole body. We found that you were just exactly perfect, just what we wanted. Mommy and Daddy were so happy that they thanked God again and again for giving them such a beautiful baby."

Now, obviously, this story will have to be tailored to fit each situation. Couples who were not at all delighted at the thought of having a child will have to concentrate their positive remarks on how beautiful and perfect the baby was when it came. No child should ever have the feeling that it was not wanted. Stay as positive as possible. Let your child experience feelings of preciousness and specialness—which *each* child *is*, regardless of how the parents felt.

The narrative will also have to be changed for an adopted child. The desire and the delight can still be there. Wanting to have a baby in the family is also good news. The discussion of having to seek a baby when having one's own was not possible can proceed to finding a precious baby who did not have a mommy and daddy to take care of him/her.

"Sometimes, Hector, women have babies they cannot take care of themselves, and because they love them so much, they want them to have the very best home possible. So they *relinquish* that baby to a couple who can *give* the best care."

Never use the phrase "gave you away." A relinquishing mother can more easily be seen as a caring, thoughtful person who had the best interests of her baby at heart, even though it was hard for her to let someone else take care of him/her. (Explanatory words for *relinquish* might be "looked

INFANTS AND CHILDREN ARE SEXUAL TOO 17

for a better home," "asked people to help her find good parents for her baby," or "placed you in a home with both a loving mommy and daddy.")

Out-of-wedlock parents have another situation to consider. Some have felt that if their child knows that she/he was conceived or born before marriage, this will cause loss of respect or provide a wrong model. That possibility always exists, of course, and must be considered as one of the consequences of making love before marriage. However, since the child probably cannot be protected from ever hearing the truth on this matter, it is usually better for the parents to address it than have the child surmise or find out from others. Many parents in this situation, however, have found their child very understanding and able to cope with this information when it is provided in a loving, open atmosphere.

Sometimes this explanation may come when the child first notices discrepancies in statistical information. Some parents talk this over with their children when they first initiate talk on dating values, if it has not come up before then. It is quite probable that having gone through the months of pregnancy under less than ideal circumstances brought with it some concern and even embarrassment. Sharing this could help their child realize how much better it would have been for so many people if they had followed God's timetable for their sexuality.

Above all, what must come through loud and clear is that they love this child, regardless of circumstances. They may want to voice the hope that this son or daughter will be making good decisions about future sexuality that will protect him or her from the distress that they (the parents) experienced.

If children see the wrong kinds of sex (e.g., outside of marriage or unfaithfulness) on TV, how can we as parents teach them the truth?

A simplistic answer would be, get rid of the TV set! But it is not as easy as that. Since our children are bombarded with sexual stimuli from other people's sets and other media, it sometimes seems a losing battle to try to preserve a sense of fidelity and dignity in the area of sexuality. But let us remember that our children's minds are ours to impress long before they get into the neighborhood and schools, and we are responsible for our own TV dials. It is during these precious years that we can be giving them the correct information, putting God right into the middle of all sexuality, where He belongs. This will have a lasting influence. We have the right and responsibility to protect our homes from television that is offensive. We cannot accomplish this by preaching gloom and doom. We have to have a substitute for what it offers. Family times need to be enhanced and made pleasurable.

Acceptable television programs can be watched together and then discussed together. Let me repeat *discussed*. After an episode is over, we can talk about what was depicted. Did we feel comfortable with the language used? What about the action—did we agree with the behaviors of the players? What choices would we have made under similar circumstances? If parents don't have time to do this, perhaps the amount of watching should be curtailed to what can be discussed. Don't plan on a joyous acceptance of this new order of television viewing! But parents are not running popularity contests. They are attempting to rear young people who can make good choices and sort the chaff from the wheat.

Family prayers could include not only requesting the usual blessings—safety, forgiveness, etc.—but also asking for a band of angels to protect the children from the moral problems around them. Children can hear us ask our heavenly Father to help them make good choices about their sexuality. Hearing us ask God to work for the greatest happiness in their lives by heeding His plan for their sexuality—as well as other areas of their lives—cannot but have an effect on their decisions.

Aren't you afraid that sex education will get out of control?

It already has! Sex education provided by television, radio, music lyrics, misinformed peers—all this is sex education, and it is out of control! Homes where there are no love and warmth demonstrated between parents, and between parents and children, are also out of control. This causes young people to seek warmth and loving attentions from other sources. When we try to teach sex education as merely a recitation of biological process, we are also losing out. Sex education must be within the bounds of God's plan, which is beautiful and regulated. We do not have to worry about telling our children about their bodies and body functions when we present these with God's moral guidelines as a basis. Someone has said, "Truth does not corrupt; lack of truth corrupts." I heartily agree. Let's add, information does not promote experimentation—lack of information does.

Speaking of Masturbation

Please explain the term *masturbation*.

This is a subject that can stir up a great deal of controversy. Since this behavior is not mentioned in the Bible (and all careful Christian scholars agree on this), we sometimes find it difficult to sort out the ideas surrounding the broad topic of masturbation. First of all, let us point out what masturbation is not.

It is not the curious exploring of infants and small children as they become acquainted with their bodies. Nothing is more natural than for these little ones to have an inquisitive interest in each part of their bodies. They use the skills of touching—the same skills which are not questioned when other parts of their bodies are being "studied." To punish, to firmly push hands away, or to talk in stern disapproval only calls attention to this part of the body, rather than deflecting interest from it.

Masturbation is not synonymous with nocturnal emissions, or what is often known as "wet dreams." This is an involuntary release of seminal fluid sometimes experienced by males as a release from sexual tension. Too often boys have been shamed and accused of dark deeds when their bodies have assumed this function. Sometimes young men suffer needless guilt and remorse when they have an emission in their sleep and have been made to feel that this is an evidence of impurity. They must be accurately educated to understand that this is God's way of providing release from sexual tension. And they should know about it before the time that it could happen in their bodies, to prevent surprise and fear.

Masturbation is not something husbands and wives do to each other. One sometimes reads the term *mutual masturbation*, which is really a contradictory term. Masturbation does not include a man and woman stimulating one another's bodies.

Masturbation is an act of self-stimulation to the point of sexual climax, or orgasm. It is usually employed to release sexual tension and provide sexual gratification. It is a solo activity involving the body of the person undertaking this behavior. Perhaps this is one of the reasons it offends the sensibilities of many people. Since sexual intercourse was intended to be bodily communication between a husband and wife, they feel that it should be reserved for this relationship-enhancing role that God planned for it. Sexuality misses the mark when it is cheated of this communion, this sharing and joining.

What do you tell a little boy when you notice that he likes to handle his penis and play with himself (about three to five years old)?

In the discussion earlier, we noted that children learn to explore their bodies naturally. In the course of their exploration, they will probably discover that touching their genitals feels better than touching their elbows or toes. With more nerve endings in these sensitive areas, that would seem only natural. Sometimes when our little ones feel lonely, bored, or frightened, if they sense disapproval or experience impatience, one would expect them to reach for the best feeling that they know about, to compensate. If at this time they are reprimanded or punished, they feel even more perturbed and instead of getting rid of this behavior, it is unconsciously encouraged.

Perhaps your little boy has sometimes felt these feelings—as almost every child certainly has. Maybe because of your feelings about masturbation, you have given negative messages. You may want to check his environment. Has he recently been "replaced" by a new sibling? Could he be experiencing lack of emotional and intellectual stimulation? Does his father provide time for playing, reading, tussling?

When you notice your little boy touching his genitals, take

INFANTS AND CHILDREN ARE SEXUAL TOO　　　　　　　21

him on your lap and tell him that you notice that he is playing with his penis. "It probably feels good, doesn't it? Do you like to do that when you need a good feeling? You know, Hector, Mommy would like to hug you and tell you how much she loves you when you are feeling sad [or lonely, or upset, or tired, etc.]. Mommy also wants to tell you that it is not appropriate to be touching your penis when other people are around. This is a special, private part of your body, and we are asking you not to do this in company. When we are home alone, just come to Mommy or Daddy and tell us what will make you feel good when you need us."

Don't expect immediate changes in behavior. But if you persist in giving this little fellow lots of demonstrated love and caring, and if you read to him and sing to him before naps and bedtime, it will give him a sense of security. If your husband—or an uncle or grandparent—can spend time with him playing games, tumbling on the grass, or doing "gymnastics" on the rug, I believe you will notice a difference in his behavior. Above all, don't make him feel that he is a bad boy. This is why I choose to use the word *appropriate* rather than *naughty* or *dirty*. We teach our children that there are many things not "appropriate" when they are around others—picking their noses, spitting, etc. It is a great word for helping our youngsters learn what society will accept in their behavior and what will alienate them from others.

One more suggestion. Be sure that there are no physical reasons why he touches his penis unduly. There could be an irritation caused by any of several physical problems. You may want to have that checked. Be sure his clothes are not restricting and tugging at his crotch. This can sometimes be the reason why he pulls on his clothes, which may look like penis-play.

> **I am a lower-division Sabbath School leader. Sometimes in Sabbath School a little girl will have her hand under her dress or in her thighs. Usually I will say quietly (and pull her dress down at the same time), "Here, let's put your dress down." Is this inappropriate or wrong?**

I think you are handling this situation very well in not making the little girl feel disapproved of, naughty, or bad. Perhaps you can begin next week by welcoming her with a special hug or commendation and then involve her in the Sabbath School program as much as you can. Other class teachers can be alerted to be especially giving to this little one.

Here you can use the "A" word again! "You know, in Sabbath School it is not *appropriate* to do this," as you move her hand. Another of the dangers of allowing her to continue this behavior is that in being noticed by other children, she may be laughed at or ignored. You can see how this would intensify her need to find some physical gratification. Sometimes the best thing we can do to help these children whom we see for such a short time each week is to teach them what is appropriate and what others will accept in public. That's not enough, but it's at least one step.

Some may wonder why I am not suggesting that you talk to her parents about this. My fear in doing that would be that they might punish her because of their own embarrassment, and that would only make the situation worse for her. Depending on how well you know the parents and how receptive you think they would be, you could make the decision that you will talk to them and explain how you are handling this situation. It might give them a clue for their own response.

At the time of the birth of my children, we were not Adventists, and I thought masturbation was normal. Several years later, I was educated by E. G. White on the harmful effects. Now we have discussed this with our children and prayed with them. It seems that one is still struggling, and so am I. What else can we do?

I appreciate your conscientious desire to be on the right side of this question. Many others are puzzled about the difference in convictions about masturbation. I believe the topic needs to be understood more broadly. There are different types of masturbation. Accidental masturbation is when a person, without having deliberately sought stimulation, comes upon it in the course of another activity. For some,

INFANTS AND CHILDREN ARE SEXUAL TOO

that has been riding a bike or climbing a tree. There is masturbation of curiosity, which may be suggested by a peer and carried out from a desire to find out what it is all about. Masturbation can then be continued from either of these beginnings, because it serves a purpose to relieve feelings of loneliness, depression, or inadequacy. Persons find that the "rush" of adrenalin temporarily makes them feel better. Guilt may then be felt, to the extent that another "rush" is needed to get rid of the guilt feelings—and so on! This may be an occasional or rather frequent experience.

When a person becomes dependent on these "highs" to the extent that he/she prefers them to social contact with others or other activities, we become justly concerned. We would say that a person with this much felt need for the "rushes" that masturbation provides would be experiencing sexual obsession or addiction. Though our present culture rarely sees masturbation as a deeply significant problem, therapists do become concerned when any sexual need or act invades every other part of a person's life.

Now let's get back to the Ellen White material which you were referring to. You may have noticed that she never used the term *masturbation*, even though the word was an established part of the vocabulary at the time that she wrote. She used instead very negative terms like secret vice and *self-abuse*. Her culture was more aggressive against this practice than she was. Some of the measures parents were instructed in by the then-current literature sound abusive today. They included tying children to their beds "spread-eagled" on their backs, with each foot and hand tied to a different corner of the bedstead. Little wire cages were put on a boy's genitals so that he could not touch them. If the penis became erect even in sleep, it would be stung by the sharp points designed to cut into the flesh of an erect penis. Sometimes cauterization of the penis was suggested. Parents were told that it would be better for their sons to visit prostitutes than to masturbate. Well-to-do homes would employ a sitter to be by the bedside of their children all night to make sure that they were always sleeping on their backs with both hands above the covers. Ellen White's remarks seem rather temperate by these standards!

Some people subscribe to the theory that Ellen White didn't know what she was talking about when she made her statements about "secret vice," etc. They believe that she was simply reflecting the ideas of her day. But then we are reminded that Ellen White was frequently medically correct when all those around her rejected her words. It seems, then, that we are faced with this choice. Either Ellen White didn't know what she was talking about, or *we* don't know what she was talking about. I believe that she was talking about masturbation that would today be called obsessive or addictive.

Now let me make this clear: I believe that God's ideal for sexual expression is an act to be consummated between a loving wife and husband in a committed, exclusive, and till-death-do-us-part relationship. Anything else in the way of sexual behavior falls short of that ideal. But I also believe that by using scare tactics to present masturbation as almost the unpardonable sin, we have turned off many young people and have actually turned some away.

I would rather see a balanced look at this issue. We point our children to the ideal, but when they fall short of God's goal for sexuality, He is the same loving, understanding God as He is when *we* fall short of His goal for making the Sabbath a delight or having a mouth with no guile or in manifesting kindness and love to our families.

Are sexual abuse and incest becoming more common, or is society just talking about it more?

Probably both. With the sexual revolution and our willingness to discuss sexual aspects more freely, many children and formerly abused persons have come forward to share their painful experiences. Children are being given permission to ask for help when they are caught in this tragic situation.

However, with the rising divorce rates, remarriages, and blending of stepchildren and stepparents, social scientists believe that more molestation is taking place. The taboo to be sexual with one's own child is stronger than the proscription against sexual behavior with a stepchild, who is not seen as a blood relative. While parent-child molestation is frequently reported, stepparent activity is more frequent. Male perpetra-

INFANTS AND CHILDREN ARE SEXUAL TOO

tors greatly outnumber their female counterparts, but it would be incorrect to give the impression that women are not also involved with their sons, stepsons, or younger brothers. Older brothers are also included as perpetrators, as well as male relatives—grandfathers, uncles, cousins and live-in boyfriends.

Persons who have been molested themselves in childhood or youth seem more likely to fall into this pattern when they become adults. That is why it is so important for perpetrators to be identified and treated. What seems to be involved here is lack of positive sex education, a poor self-concept, and not understanding how to properly express affection.

Until the last few decades, children who reported to their mothers that they had been molested did not get a good ear. Many women have later given an account of their mothers' responses. One person writes, "I told my mother about it for six years, and she wouldn't believe me. She said it was in my thoughts."

"When my grandfather started to bother me, my mother would say, 'Be understanding. Grandma and Grandpa haven't slept together for ___ years, and Grandpa is lonely. Remember, he loves you.' "

Another states, "My dad told me that this was what all fathers did to teach their daughters how to be wives when they got married."

I wish I could say that these were atypical responses, but they are all too representative of many others.

In our wish to keep things looking good in our homes, schools, and churches, we have tried to cover up unsavory reports, or pray away these incidents as though everything would then be all right. It's time we realized that we are each responsible for these little ones. When we are faced with evidence or actual knowledge of this kind of abuse, we must be involved in reporting to the correct authorities. This would be the Child Protective Services in any county of the United States.

Reporting is not an underhanded, unchristian thing to do. It is an opportunity for the family to find out what is wrong in its system and work to correct that for the betterment of *each* person in the family, including the perpetrator. It can preserve the victim from further violation and begin a treatment course that will seek to minimize the terrible consequences that can affect the child's life for many years to come. It is not meddling. It is mending.

How can little girls be reassured after sexual abuse?

They must be told, repeatedly, that it was *not* their fault. They did nothing wrong, but what the *person* who hurt them did was wrong, *wrong*, WRONG! One of the most prevailing feelings that these girls grow up with is that they in some way invited what happened to them, and that they are bad, and to use their own word, "dirty."

Whether the perpetrator was outside the family or inside the family, it is important to seek professional help. Child Protective Services almost always has specially trained persons who know just how to help these unfortunate ones work through their memories, their hang-ups, and their fears. This can even be done many years later, after the fact. Specially formed resources are designed to provide help and support to victims. Every possible means of therapy should be employed to mend the damage, including individual, marital, family, and group work. Families must rally round and make these children feel especially loved, cherished, and protected.

With the recent increase in reporting child abuse, do you believe there is a danger in children falsely accusing a parent or a relative or a neighbor for ulterior motives?

Nothing is impossible. But I would say that this happens in only a very few cases. In the first place, when this is reported, as it should be, the professionals who talk to the child are usually well trained. They know how to frame questions and comments so that the child will trip herself/himself up if it is a planted idea or a vengeful one. Small children especially would not be able to conjure up the words to report this kind of incident. Children would be much less likely to have "ulterior motives" than adults would. I feel that

INFANTS AND CHILDREN ARE SEXUAL TOO

a child should be believed and given the benefit of the doubt. The reporting should be done.

Please remember, reporting is not the same as "going out to get someone." In the long run, reporting can be a positive thing for a whole family system. It can also be the means of warning careless people in our neighborhoods that roving hands and suggestive actions are not welcome. It may prevent something worse from happening in the future.

How do you endeavor to watch for signs/signals of sexual abuse in children?

In infants and children who cannot talk, we watch for redness and irritation of the genitals. A child pulling at these parts of the body unduly could also suggest that this part of the body is being disturbed. A youngster may also show evidence of irregular and disturbed sleep patterns, irritability, anxiety, and fear. Older toddlers may have an unusual interest in the genitals of other children or the adults around her/him.

Older children who can share their experiences verbally can also manifest some of these same symptoms. In addition, they may try to tell us what is happening with language or actions that may sometimes be baffling—that is, unless we have taught them the correct names for body parts and a respect for their bodies. We must prepare our children by instructing them to say a loud "NO" to anyone who touches the special/private parts of their bodies. This is especially necessary since we usually tell them that they must do what adults tell them to do—almost any adult from Grandpa to a store clerk.

Often the child will be told by the perpetrator not to tell when he/she has been molested, or something terrible will happen to both of them, and the child will be responsible. Thus children are wooed into keeping "our little secret." Each of these messages plays right into the child's thinking and often accounts for her/him not telling for some time.

In these older children we would also look for symptoms such as sleep disorders (sleeplessness, nightmares, sleepwalking); change in school performance and behavior patterns around others; fear and clinging; not wanting to be near certain people who may heretofore have been acceptable; changes in personality (a child who has been sunny and cooperative becomes sad or morose, a talkative child becomes quiet, a mischievous one become strangely over-compliant). One could go on with distinct changes in behavior, but this gives an idea of what to look for.

Caution: These behaviors do not always indicate molestation or incest. But they deserve some concern and attention, whatever the source, and this should be one of the areas of exploration.

Someone said that being in the delivery room and involved with the birth is a deterrent to a potentially abusive father. Is this valid?

This interesting viewpoint follows surveys in this area. It seems like a reasonable result of feeling deeply parental and responsible for a little one. Since it has many other good results for family bonding and cohesion, I heartily recommend it as a wonderful love experience for the couple and their baby.

What steps can be taken to be reunited as a family after a child has been abused and now as an adult completely refuses any communication with either parent?

This sad question demonstrates the deep feelings of resentment and anger that a child feels long after having been abused. I don't know what attempts have been made to try to get communication started between these alienated family members. But if reconciliation is to be successful, it must certainly start with a full confession by the perpetrator along with a willingness to assume full responsibility for what happened. The confession must be actually verbalized, not left as an assumption that the victim should know. The perpetrator must be willing to listen to all the anger and resentment that have festered through the years without offering extenuating circumstances or finding excuses. There must be a specific acknowledgement of specific wrongs. This may be a very humbling experience, but so be it. Forgiveness must be sought. God can provide the grace.

INFANTS AND CHILDREN ARE SEXUAL TOO

Home Modesty

What is your view regarding children viewing parents naked or showering together . . . should you stop this at a certain age?

One thing we are now realizing is that children are not as asexual as we used to think they were. Formerly we thought that the age of pubescence was the time when children began to have sexual ideas and feelings. We know better now. Very small children can be sexually stimulated by what they see. Since we live in a culture that sexualizes everything, children are bombarded with suggestive stimuli and are much more sexually aware, much younger than we realize.

Some authorities feel that by ages three to five years, children should be spared the stimulation of seeing their opposite-sex parent naked. Some even suggest that parents should discontinue bathing their opposite-sex child around that time.

Often children themselves let us know when they wish to observe more modesty. This should be honored. Children should never be teased when they begin to wish for more body privacy. Youngsters may inadvertently come across their parents unclothed, and certainly this should not be treated as a federal offense! Simply a reminder that you will be ready when you get some clothes on is usually enough. When children become preoccupied with the genitals of others, even under three years, it may be an indication that more modesty is appropriate. This undue curiosity may also mean that children are curious about something that has never been named or explained to them. Children have a right to expect their parents to answer all their sexual questions. In fact, one study indicated that when asked, children stated that they would rather have their parents tell them about sex than anyone else. Unfortunately, those same children reported that they got most of their sex information from other sources—which got ahead of their parents!

At what age should a child stop sleeping with his or her parent of the opposite sex—whether in the same room or in the same bed?

As soon as possible after birth. Both parents and children usually sleep better when they have their own beds to roll and toss in. It is downright dangerous to sleep with an infant, for it is too easy to roll over the little one and crush it. But aside from this, a child should not make a habit of sleeping with its parent for other reasons. It interrupts the loving and cuddling that is so important for Mom and Dad, especially when the child takes so much time and attention during the day. Couples need time alone. A better plan to promote bedroom closeness is to invite the children to sit on the bed while reading the bedtime story or to come in for a few moments of togetherness on a morning when it works into the rising time of the family members.

Naturally there will be "bad-dream" times when a child will want to run in to the parents' bed for comfort. But after soothing and reassuring, the child should be returned to his/her own bed so that the habit, which is sometimes so hard to break, does not get started.

Is it right to engage in sexual intercourse in the presence of your children?

An unqualified No. The sexual embrace of a man and a woman is to be in privacy. That was one of the circumstances that made the first sexual experience in the Garden of Eden so ideal. Other advantages Adam and Eve had included a setting of great beauty, a relationship of equality, and a complete surety that God approved of their marital love experience.

What parents do when they make love does not look very loving to a little child. It can give the impression of overpowering and hurting. Even very loving intercourse can be very puzzling to a child. However, when this "primal scene" is inadvertently discovered, the best response should be calm and reassuring. Explain that Mommy and Daddy were playing together and having a loving time—which is something that only mommies and daddies do. Lots of loving reassurance is in order, both when it happens and again the next day.

What do you do when you find your children playing "Mommy and Daddy" with one another or a neighbor's children?

INFANTS AND CHILDREN ARE SEXUAL TOO

Almost every parent comes upon this situation at one time or another. Becoming angry and shocked is *not* the way to handle it, although it may be the most natural response. Children usually have no idea that they are doing something that will be so disturbing to their parents, at least the first time, and can be genuinely puzzled and distressed by the parental reaction.

It is usually a good idea to ask first what they are doing and find out how they see their behavior. This should be followed by a quiet and pleasant command to get their clothes back on, with some gentle assistance. During this time you can explain that it is not appropriate to play with their clothes off. We wear clothes to protect our bodies from injury, as well as to provide warmth and sexual designation. Suggesting other ways to play the "Mommy-Daddy" game, or another activity, can take care of this episode.

Chapter 2

Teens Have Questions About the "S" Word

What an exciting time to be a teenager! And what a bewildering time! Don't let anyone tell you that things were just as tough when they were your age. As far as dealing with sexuality is concerned, today you have all the enticements we had, plus many more. The sale of sexuality has invaded our entire commercial system. Add to these confusing feelings the easy availability of drugs, living under the shadow of an atomic holocaust, and, don't forget, homes breaking up at a record number. Put that all together, and that's a lot to cope with at the same time you are going through the developmental stage with tasks of finding your identity and learning to be more independent.

Generally, we adults have not been too helpful at reasonable dialogue about sexuality between the two generations. Too often we have lectured rather than explained, threatened rather than discussed, and ignored rather than spent time sharing our own experience and working through problems with you. I hope we are beginning to improve.

The following questions are only a small sample of the mound I have sorted out from teens. But I think they will demonstrate that what is going on in your mind is pretty much the same as what young folks everywhere are puzzling over. Let me thank you for the questions you entrusted me with. The questions are sorted into six categories. Let's start with the ones which deal with boy-girl concerns and discovering one another.

Boy-Girl Relationships

> If this guy writes you a note and tells you that he cares about you, but he never talks to you, what are you supposed to do?

It must feel good to know that one of your schoolmates finds you attractive and cares about you. Of course you would like him to follow through with opportunities to talk and get acquainted. He probably feels the very same way and would love to be able to saunter up and easily slip into a fascinating conversation. But he may fear that you will not be interested in talking with him. He may be afraid that he won't come across right and that he will do something that will turn you off. (Be sure to read the questions following this one.) It's not easy to be the initiator either, especially when you are new at it or have had a bad experience in the past when you did try.

When you see this young man, you can be friendly and spend a bit more time in saying "Hi" and adding a bit of small talk yourself. You may even want to thank him for his note, if he is alone and won't be embarrassed by your mentioning it. Maybe he will get the idea that you are open to a special friendship with him. I would discourage a "notes only" friendship, since that won't give either one of you the chance to get acquainted. This is one of the real advantages of boy-girl friendships, learning to listen and talk to one another. Girls sometimes develop their social skills somewhat sooner than their male peers do, so be friendly—and patient!

Two fellows will present the other side of the coin in the next two questions.

What if you like some girl but are too shy to tell her or go near her because she hangs around a bunch of other girls? And if you do, you would be afraid of making a scene, or of her laughing at you or telling you to get lost.

What can you do if you like someone and usually you manage to act stupid around them when you don't want to?

It's really tough to feel unsure in your behavior when you are around someone of the opposite sex, especially when you are just beginning to want to have a special friendship with them. You probably look about you and get the idea that everyone you are observing seems to have so much poise and know-how. Don't be fooled! Underneath a lot of bravado is often the same kind of shaky, insecure feelings that you two have pictured in your questions.

Being shy can sometimes be very painful, but fortunately it is not fatal and very rarely lasts forever. When you are around this young lady, try to ==stop worrying about your looks== and ==concentrate more on finding out about her==. You'll find you are more likely to forget your own discomfort and come out great! ==Have a few starters in mind for beginning a conversation==, like: "What do you think about what the principal said today about the new social rules?" or "I noticed in class you really seemed good at that new algebra unit," or "You look good in blue. I notice you wear it a lot, and I like it on you."

By the law of averages, you may be turned down and laughed at sometimes. You see, girls are new at this kind of thing too and may not always act appropriately. You may also continue to do stupid things occasionally—join the club! But that is all in the interest of learning and becoming. Keeping at it will soon help you to loosen up and be more comfortable. Develop a sense of humor about the whole thing. Believe it or not, someday you will get a good laugh about some of the things that are happening to you now in learning social skills—someday! Just store those incidents up, and later in college you may be able to charm some young lady by telling her about your bungling!

Can you be in love with two or three people at the same time?

That would depend on how you define love. If you mean being attracted to, wanting to be near, getting a heart-throb-rush every time you are together—yes, it is possible. This is the time of life when you are trying out different feelings about opposite-sex persons. Sometimes the feeling for them may come fast and furious, sometimes one after another, and sometimes one on top of another! These emotions are not necessarily a signal to get serious, but still you can enjoy and learn from them.

Now, I am certain that if one of your parents were asking

you the same questions about themselves, you would be quite concerned! We expect different kinds of responses from adult, married love—and we have a right to. We define that kind of love in a different way, and it makes other demands on the persons involved. That's good to remember as your emotions continue to develop.

As long as you don't commit yourself to a steady relationship with one person, it's perfectly OK to enjoy the friendships of two or more people to whom you feel attracted.

I find myself attracted to this one boy, but he is a total jerk. What do I do?

First of all, let me commend you on being able to admit that he is a "total jerk" when at the same time you feel attracted to him. Some less thoughtful young lady might try to defend and make excuses for his "jerkiness" and roll along in the relationship anyway. But let's admit that even a total jerk may have something about him that can be appealing. Maybe he attracts you because he reminds you of someone else, or you are excited by his way of looking at you, or perhaps he has a great way with words. When you figure out what it might be that is so appealing, you will be in a better position to understand your response to him.

This might be a really good time to sharpen your pencil and jot down on a piece of paper a list of what you think *is* important to you in a young man. Go for the best in this list; there is nothing wrong with being idealistic. Then when you feel an attraction for this "one guy," remind yourself of your list, and remind yourself that you are not going to spend time getting involved with someone who appears so unpromising.

At the same time I am saying this, I would want you to realize that some "total jerks" may be young men who realize that they do stupid things around girls and wish they were more in control. Sometimes they even grow up to be fine men.

But you know better than I do what caused your evaluation. If his values and goals are lacking, if his sense of responsibility is nil, if his language and its contents are turn-offs, and if he treats people badly, he may well be a totally inappropriate person to spend time with now. Boy-girl friendships are not intended to be rescue missions or reform sessions. Perhaps the best thing to do is let him work out his problems outside of your time.

Why is it that you can't be popular with the boys unless you have a perfect figure and a pretty face? We put up with *their* looks!

It's true that attractive physical features in a girl are higher on a fellow's list than on a girl's list. But it is generally not tops on either list! A *good personality* is usually most important, and that is something anyone can learn to achieve, whether he/she has a head start or not. These are some qualities that people have told me first led them to their future wife or husband: friendliness, being easy to talk to, lots of pep and energy, looking like they are fun to be with, a good reputation, and yes—attractiveness and looking good. By looking good, they mean that regardless of other endowments, they are squeaky clean, neat, tastefully dressed, and well groomed.

You may not be able to do much to achieve perfection in face and figure, but you sure can do a lot about the rest of those qualities. You might want to look around at some of the married people you know. Not all the wives are beauty pageant winners. Some may even be quite plain. But as you notice their interaction with others, you can usually understand why their husbands thought they were good marriage material. What we are inside can impart a sense of beauty to the outer person. Mysterious, but true.

I like this guy and we were really close until we messed around a little, and now he doesn't talk with me. But I still like him a lot. What should I do—try not to like him anymore or keep trying? I'm really confused.

Although you do not define "messed around a little," I am going to assume that you mean that you got involved in some types of hugging, kissing, and perhaps sexual touching. Probably if you were doing some conscious thinking about it at the time, you felt that this was an indication of caring and a way to hang on to the relationship. Now you may be really disappointed and perhaps even upset with yourself for going along with it. What makes it worse for you is his seeming rejection of you now. Of course you are confused.

Maybe he is confused too. Maybe he had as a value not to get into necking and petting now and is blaming himself, or maybe even you, for the situation. Perhaps he had no idea that he would want to "duck out" on feelings that may have been more intense than he intended. On the other hand, this may be his way of carrying on his relationships, a "love-em and leave-em" kind of person. We hope not, but we will have to admit that there are some of these kinds of people, both boys and girls.

It seems you don't have many choices here. You will have to accept that at this time he doesn't want to continue the friendship. When you see him, you can still tell him Hi, but protect yourself from further hurt and confusion by trying on your own to get things going again.

Perhaps you have learned something very valuable. Both of you are not ready to deal with the emotional overlay of "messing around." For a few years, keep your future relationships on a less-involved level, concentrating on learning to understand each other's ideas, interest, values, and goals. Learn how to be a good friend first. When you eventually marry, you'll want it to be to someone who has practiced all these fine qualities of friendship too. That makes the best marriages, believe me!

What do you do when you now have a girlfriend but still have feelings for your last one? These feelings come like waves. Especially after a fight with your current one.

Each close and meaningful relationship we have results in a certain bonding between us. Usually it requires a termination process for us to let go of the emotions we felt for that person. People who have studied this have even defined the steps in the process that we go through when we have experienced a loss, so it is very real. Even if you were eager to be out of the other relationship, you would still go through the process of separating. Perhaps you had not finished doing this when you started your new relationship. It may even be that your sense of loss pushed you prematurely into this new friendship. That may not have been the best reason to get into something new.

When a relationship has ended, generally it is a good time to stop and evaluate what your attraction for one another consisted of, how you two got along, and what caused the breakup. Each time you go with someone, you should learn from that experience how to increase your skills of getting along with others and how to be a good friend. Even if you did all these things, you might still feel a tug in the tummy at certain times when your old relationship comes to mind. It may not help to hear the old adage, "Time heals all wounds." But I will tell you something that could help and is often good to remember. We are made to heal. God made us to miraculously mend in both body and spirit—isn't that just like God?

If there's a guy you like and the two of you are friends but argue a lot—because of selfishness, stubbornness, or just plain immaturity on both parts—but you both like each other deep down inside, do you think it's wise to pursue this relationship beyond a friendship?

Fighting and arguing indicate that two people have not learned to deal with differences, impulses, and anger—among other things. You are smart to be concerned about it. It doesn't go away by itself. Time is no cure. Some people come from families where arguing is so much a part of the family's operating style that it is only natural to handle almost any aggravation by arguing. Some seek to protect themselves from a lack of self-esteem. Not feeling "in the right" is threatening, so they argue to prove their point. Others are so basically angry at the world and themselves that the least annoyance will start an argument.

You sound like you might be able to talk to your friend about this and wonder together what is happening. Try to figure out some kind of a buzz-word or phrase you can use to call "time out" to an argument, and then learn what you can about it right then. Now, if your friend thinks this is silly and a lot of work, maybe your relationship should not go beyond a friendship. That wouldn't be a good sign for you how you are going to improve your interaction. Keep your sights on someone more even-tempered, who is looking for less fireworks and more peace!

What would you do if a girl went with you for a short time, then dropped you, then came back, and then dropped you again? Is there something wrong with me? It really hurts.

I'm sure it does. People have told me about so much pain they have experienced in the course of dating and breaking up that sometimes I wonder if there isn't something wrong with a system that causes this to happen over and over again. Your question again shows the changeable feelings of young people your age and serves as a real caution to relationships that bring a boy and girl too close together, emotionally or physically. There is probably nothing wrong with you, except perhaps you expected too much, too young. There may not be anything "wrong" with her, either, except perhaps a thoughtlessness that is common at your age. I wonder if some of this pain could be avoided if we looked at dating differently than we do. But that is the subject of the next section, so read on.

What About Dating?

Just a word before the questions. Dating is a particularly modern and American social form. When people lived in rural communities (as they still do in much of the world) and hardly ever went more than a few miles from home in a lifetime, they knew all about everyone in the area. Parents then would arrange their marriages, often considering the desires of the young people, and there were not many surprises. You knew in advance if your new spouse was a loner, a good worker, a clown, a tightwad, a yeller, whatever.

As time went on and people moved into cities to be close to factories and other workplaces, it became necessary to find some way to get young people together so they could find out enough about one another to make a marriage choice. Voila! Dating was created.

In the past few decades, dating has taken on new dimensions. What started out to be a helpful device sometimes now has turned out to be a competitive game. Either you're involved in it, or you feel left out. This makes a push for closeness between two people, which may be all wrong. Result: separation, then starting over again and wondering what will happen next.

I would rather think of dating as an opportunity to learn what you need to know about yourself and others. Eventually you will be able to choose a good marriage partner. Then you need to realize that the more dating you do on a friendship level, the more valuable marriage training you can gain. What are some of the things you will learn? How to get along with different types of people; how to be sensitive to the other person's viewpoint; how to disagree without being disagreeable; how to share feelings; how to understand differences of opposite-sex persons; how to find qualities in a relationship that will make you a better person—for starters! The more people who have an opportunity to know others in this way, the better are the chances to gain really important maturity. If dating is seen only as a recreational game, if it is only a time to get close physically, it is not doing its job! Now for your questions.

What do you think is an ideal age for a young person to begin dating?

First of all, I don't know from the question what kind of dating you are asking about. If it is family dating, where your "date" accompanies you and your family on some family outing, we have a totally different picture than if it is an unaccompanied, unsupervised date. Many schools and churches have activities that bring boys and girls together in a sort of friendship-dating social event. These sorts of recreationals are often planned for early teens. I wish there were more of them. I also wish that while they are enjoying them, the young people could realize the good fun they can have without planning to come, stay, and go with the same person.

Dating that becomes steady or exclusive really demands a certain level of maturity from those taking part. Parents and older Christian adults can usually identify this maturity in a teenager. They will look for: someone who can keep promises about schedules; teens willing to have an open discussion on plans and activities without attempts to deceive; someone who has a fair sense of responsibility with money, about driver's licenses, and about promises; and someone who is sensitive to the feelings of others. They will also look for young people who have made beginning decisions about their future and have beginning plans to get there—such as holding down a part-time job, saving money, and helping with some of their own expenses. A mature person is someone who keeps school grades at a level satisfactory to themselves as well as parents and teachers (this may not mean all A's, but it will give evidence of making good effort). Most parents would probably accept this young person as mature enough to be ready for steady dating.

So you see, it is not so much a matter of chronological age as of where one is on the maturity scale. Perhaps a look at yourself will help you to see if you are ready for the fun—and responsibility—of dating.

I have been advised that while I am still single, I ought to date as many girls as I can, because I won't be able to after I am married. It gives me a guilty feeling to date a different girl every week.

That guilty feeling probably comes from the prevailing philosophy that dating means settling in, rather than having fun. Many teens have penned their negative feelings about this attitude. They resent the notion that if they date someone one time, everyone takes it for granted that they are ready to fall in love. Here's one person's apt comment about this: "It's ridiculous!"

Now, I can understand a young person's offense at this kind of behavior if a person takes on a crusade to date a different person every week just for the sake of setting a record! But if there is an honest desire to meet as many people as possible during this independent time of life, go for it! It would be unfair in this type of dating to pretend seriousness or to expect behaviors that go with steady dating, of course.

How do you tell a guy to get lost without hurting his feelings? (It could also be a girl—some girls can also be pretty persistent!)

Maybe you can't. If someone feels very insecure and has invested a lot of energy in building up enough courage to make friendly overtures to you, some hurt may be inevitable. But I appreciate your effort not to want to hurt this person, so let's try to figure out how to make the blow the least painful.

First, you can appreciate something about them that is good—simple things like a good comment made in class, a spiritual attitude, or being friendly. Maybe even persistence! This will help to soothe a bruised ego. Perhaps you can say that not every dating couple hits it off well together, and that's how it is for you. Suggest that there are other young people in school who probably would like to have him for a special friend. You might want to soften it by suggesting he let you know how he is getting along with his search every now and then. Now you are no longer adversaries but each have the same goal, his interest in someone else.

My response to the previous question may be of some help here. If you are dating a variety of persons—and others are too—the school group will have different expectations of your dating. One could date a less popular schoolmate occasionally without getting "tagged." Sometimes these less promising people turn out to be real winners! What an advantage this could be for the kids in school who are not easily popular, but who need also to have the experience of dating. Those of us who have lived longer have met old school friends who once were told to "get lost" by someone, and that very person turned out to be surprisingly charming, attractive, and successful! Nothing brings out the potential in people like being given a chance to be accepted.

Is it appropriate for girls to ask guys for dates also?

I feel comfortable with that. It has several advantages. Girls who may have been overlooked in the present dating system have an opportunity to show that the timid-and-easy-to-over-look exterior often hides a really interesting, fun person. In addition, it helps girls see that asking for dates is not all that easy! Many times girls envy boys for the freedom they have to ask anyone, anytime. They can now experience firsthand the butterflies in the stomach, the nervous fingers on the telephone dial, and the uneasy voice that so often accompany the risky business of asking for dates. It can be plain scary!

When boys ask girls for dates, there is an assumption that they will be responsible for the finances involved. Boys sometimes find it difficult to let their dates do this, so it's a good idea to think about how you are going to handle this in advance. You may say you already have the tickets, or that this one will be on you since you happen to have inherited a fortune—whatever! This will take away that uncertainty.

How Far to Go on a Date

A large mound of questions on my desk deals with dating and physicalness. That's good. It shows that young people are thinking about this important part of dating. They really want to be on the right side of this. But the pressures and the urges are all very strong. Let's look at some of these questions.

When, in a dating life, should you begin the physical aspect of it (holding hands, hugging, etc.)?

If I knew what the "etc." in this question meant, it would help. But let's assume that the questions in this particular section are not talking about going as far as intercourse. The questioners really want to know what type of physical contact short of intercourse is appropriate and when it is all right to begin.

Again, I must say that there is no set time, no rule book that can give a formula. The urge will come, and it will come early in the relationship for most young people. Touching is a very desirable experience. Everything in your culture gives you a go-ahead signal, and your hormones cooperate quite well too!

First, let us establish that there is a progression in physical touching, and it almost invariably follows the same steps in each instance. It usually starts with hand-holding, hugging, kissing, body-touching over the clothes, body-touching under the clothes, genital touching, and intercourse. This progression should ideally take years to complete. In other words, hand-holding by itself should be such a wonderful activity that it could satisfy a young couple for months. (By the way, it is still delightful for moms and dads—it never outlives its pleasure. Isn't that good news?) Then hugging. One could spend months, even years, enjoying the closeness and companionship that this provides. That way, you see, you do not run out of pleasant contacts until you get married and are ready for the latter steps of the physical contact development.

Unfortunately, many young people don't realize that they are going so fast that they are actually shortchanging themselves on the amount of pleasure the early stages of touching are meant to provide. When you begin the physical aspects of a relationship will depend on how clearly you understand this progression and how well you can read your body signals. When your body asks for a level of touching that your head tells you is inappropriate, your maturity will take over and pull you back from behaviors which could bring unhappiness to both of you now, no matter how good or how urgent it feels momentarily. So again, it pretty much depends on your level of maturity.

Waiting is safer. Waiting is better. And waiting is also harder! But young people are usually pretty good at accepting tough challenges.

Do you think it is wrong to kiss on a date?

See the above answer and add these thoughts. There are also different kinds of kisses. There is a friendly kiss on the cheek, a light brush of the lips, a firmer kiss, and a downright passionate kiss! And again, you usually begin with the more casual-type kisses, which can quickly—very, very quickly—change into passionate ones. Perhaps you did not realize that passionate kissing is symbolic and suggestive of genital sex. This type of kissing can set bodies moving inappropriately through the stages of physical closeness.

That is why you need to know not only what you have in mind but also what your date has in mind in kissing. It's a

TEENS HAVE QUESTIONS ABOUT THE "S" WORD   45

pretty good idea to have it straight between two people dating what your expectations are of one another and what your values are as far as physical behavior is concerned. And by the way, if you *can't* talk this over with your special friend, that in itself is saying something negative about the relationship you are in.

Kissing on a date may be a pleasant and nondemanding experience, or it can be insistent and suggestive. I think I would need to know where each person in a dating pair stood on this issue before I could answer this question for you.

I've never kissed, caressed, etc., with a boy before, and I am sort of naive. Is that OK?

You are perfectly normal. Everyone does not have the same timetable for physical desire and activity. This can be a real advantage to you, for you can listen, watch, and learn before you make decisions in this important area. Many girls who have had the pain of rejection, who have "sweated out" waiting for a late period, and who have suffered through abortions would give anything to feel naive again.

How come guys persist on making moves on you, even after you have told them not to?

Let's start this by reporting that girls sometimes do the pressuring. Fellows have told me that girls have challenged them to "prove their love" too. I can't believe that this same old line is still being used. You would think it would die of old age soon! But let's get back to the girl's question.

First and foremost, the "moves" are fun; it feels good to be physically involved. Fellows also feel it is expected of them. They've been told that this is what real men are supposed to do, and they surely don't want to be considered wimps! But there is more to it than that. Some feel that dating includes fellows trying and girls resisting—and this goes on for a while till she gives in—which she really intended to do all the time, but resisting comes first! It's all part of the script.

And of course, far too often the fellows are right—it works! They think girls are just pretending not to want them to keep at their "moves." And girls sometimes play right into this by objecting with a weak, halfhearted, "Now you quit that!" in less than convincing tones. I really doubt that if a girl would say quite sternly and with great conviction, "Please do not do that to me. I am expecting you to pay attention to my wishes, or else I don't want to date you," that he'd continue. He might get mad and not want to see you again, but how much time are you willing to devote to a fellow who doesn't care about your wishes?

But maybe that would not be the result. Maybe after his profound surprise, he would be relieved that you have taken the strain off him to be a real jock. If he can then realize that he doesn't owe his friends any information at all when the date is over—that he can say just as determinedly, "Hey, man, that's my business" or a decided, "Knock it off"—what a relief it might be to him.

How do you say "No" without hurting a guy's feelings?

When we remember that most young men are doing what they think is expected of them, it helps us to realize that not all fellows are out there to get all girls. Some men *don't* want to go against the young lady's wishes and make the date a study in self-protection. The old Victorian way used to be to say, "Unhand me, you cad!" with a resounding slap on the face. A bit passé, but maybe that *should* be considered as a last resort!

When you first get your clue that this is going to be a date when (and this is how girls generally put it) "his hands are all over you," you need to act. Some comments you can adapt to your own style are: "This doesn't fit in with the way I want to run my life right now. Please don't make it hard for me to keep on my plan," or "I have made some really important decisions about physical stuff on my dates, and this goes against what I have decided," or "This kind of touching really makes me feel uncomfortable, and I am sure you wouldn't want me to feel ill at ease on a date with you." How you say this will be just as important as the words you use. If none of this stops the "pawing" (another term from one of my questions), then use a very decided, "Please stop that right

TEENS HAVE QUESTIONS ABOUT THE "S" WORD 47

now!" You don't owe anyone the right to pester and tease you about physical touching, whether you are a fellow or a girl.

I have an idea that if a majority of girls would give this kind of a message, the young men would get the idea. Some would be relieved that someone is taking over in a runaway situation. The few who are bent on pushing the borders of behavior might even get the message that this is no longer standard procedure for dating in this school, and they would have to polish up their act. What do I mean by that? It's a lot easier to plan to neck on a date than it is to be interesting, informed, and actively engaged in fun activities. But being interesting, informed, and active pays good dividends in solid relationships which are not built on physical touching.

So What's So Bad About It?

I think if you have urges, you should express them in a physical way.

Perhaps if you thought of this a little longer, you would have realized what a world we would live in if everyone did this! For instance, I live in southern California, and every now and then someone has the urge to shoot randomly at cars on the freeway. Should that type of expression be allowed? Just this past week, our newspaper printed the story of a young girl who was raped and killed because someone had the urge for violence. Would you be willing to be a good sport about someone who had the urge to gash your tires some day while you were in school or took a pair of scissors and savagely cut the long hair you had so painstakingly grown?

We do not allow expressions of any and all urges in our country. It would cause bedlam and disorganization. We have to keep some rules, hard as that may be. It is not harmful to a person to use restraint not to steal, not to murder, not to engage in inappropriate sexual behaviors. Granted, it may be unpleasant, difficult, and sometimes uncomfortable to cease and desist from these behaviors whether we have the urge or not, but it is not harmful to the person using restraint.

And when you do use sexual restraint, you are in good

company. Most young high-school students in *Who's Who* say they are waiting till they get married to have sex. They are usually the most responsible, get the best grades, and have definite plans for their futures. Many have Christian backgrounds and want to be in God's family. Not a bad group to sign up with!

OK, so we can't have intercourse now. What's so bad about doing everything but?

Young people are always eager to find out how close they can come "without." I think we need to realize that intercourse is not an event apart—it is part of a process. There are four phases of a sexual event. First there is excitement, which is signaled by an erection in the male and genital lubrication in the female. Unless some barrier to continuing exists, they are drawn further along in this desire to be close together.

The next phase is called the plateau stage, which is just a fancy word for the love play that comes before intercourse. This should be the most lengthy part of the cycle, and is characterized by pleasurable sexual touching, verbal communication of love and caring, and all those exciting things which have for their purpose preparing for the phase of intercourse and orgasm. The plateau phase is God's plan for readying the bodies of both female and male for the complete act of union. It is not a recreational pursuit for thrill seekers. The end of this stage is the orgasmic climax.

Then comes relaxation and a warm glow referred to as the resolution stage. Couples can appreciate this stage to the fullest when they can be assured that whatever the outcome of this act may be, they are ready to take responsibility for it. God's plan was that this would be a committed couple who can give to one another all the emotional, spiritual, and social support that married people can.

The big problem is this: at what point in the plateau stage does lovemaking cease to be simply a pleasurable experience and become the prelude to sexual intercourse? When two people feel so drawn to each other that they cannot continue to enjoy these initial stages of hand-holding and hugging

TEENS HAVE QUESTIONS ABOUT THE "S" WORD   49

without reaching for breasts and genitals, then they are invading marital space. If they cannot realize when this urgency becomes overpowering without pushing on heedlessly, then they are not mature enough to be engaging in any of these phases.

Dating is much more important for learning to know another's mind, values, and emotions than it is to learn about bodies—that part is easy! But the part that keeps marriages together happily and successfully is having emotional contact, truly knowing one another's minds, and feeling secure in time spent together talking, sharing, planning, understanding, and cooperating. They will spend much more time in these activities after they are married than they will in having intercourse! And when they haven't learned to know one another on the interpersonal levels and discover that sexuality on its own won't make it, they will begin to develop problems. Emotions and sexuality are so closely tied together that whatever affects one affects the other.

What if you want it but your girlfriend doesn't?

Congratulate yourself on having such a wise girlfriend! Remember, she has much more to consider than you do in premarital sex. Statistics show that only a small percentage of fellows want to marry the girls that became pregnant before marriage—not that marriage is the solution. It usually isn't.

Maybe your thoughtful girlfriend is well informed about the physical consequences such as trauma and infection, and wants to protect herself. Maybe she has heard from girls who lost part of themselves in uncommitted sex that they wish they could turn back the clock and have another chance at virginity. Maybe she is confused by information that many fellows still want to marry a "good girl" and still spend time urging the "good girls." Maybe she is a friend of the girl who previously told about having sex with her boyfriend who then dropped her.

I don't know how mature you are, but try this test: If what your girlfriend feels good about and wants is more important than what you want, *and* if you are willing to protect her feelings rather than to gratify your own, then you are becoming quite a young man. She will be a lucky girl too, to have a boyfriend like you.

Let's say someone asks you to have sex with them, and you have already explained how you feel about premarital sex. And he says he understands. Why should he keep asking you? Could it be he enjoys hearing you say "No"?

Probably not. More likely, he is hoping you will change your mind and say "Yes." Perhaps the way you said it was unsure. Maybe something you have said or done since makes him think you have changed your mind. If you have truly been firm and left no question about it, why not ask him why he keeps repeating and repeating. Maybe you both need to wonder together if your activities or the way you spend time when alone keeps bringing this into his mind.

Why do you feel that it is wrong to have premarital sex even if marriage is almost 100 percent certain?

I would like to take that word *wrong* in the above question and use the words I generally do. *Wrong* sounds very legalistic, and I think we are dealing here with something that needs less rule-making and more careful thought. I believe that it is unwise, problematic, premature, and against God's plan for assuring the best of sexuality not simply now, but later.

Marriage is never 100 percent certain until the vows are taken in front of your minister. Nearly one-third of all engagements are broken. And that was probably for the best, for they may have saved some later divorce problems. Engagement is indeed a time to explore closely and exclusively whether this relationship has what it takes for a good marriage. Leave celebration for the real thing, sealed and signed with altar promises.

Does God look bad upon premarital sex?

I believe that God looks "sad" upon premarital sex. You see,

TEENS HAVE QUESTIONS ABOUT THE "S" WORD   51

He has the highest expectations for the joy and commitment that sexual intercourse can bring to a married couple. When He sees that beautiful union, which was intended to be a symbol of Christ's everlasting love for His church, used merely to gratify urges that He meant to be under spiritual control, it must make Him very sad. When He sees the physical result of going against His plan—illness, pain, unwanted babies—it must hurt. When He sees the psychological pain resulting from overeager teens hurting one another with broken promises, and from being harmed by being forced or pressured into having unsatisfactory sexual experiences, which can leave scars, He must feel angry. When He notes all the couples marrying simply because they are sexually eager, and who have paid no attention to preparing for the other parts of their marriage relationship, He must be grieved. When He sees that, although their bodies might have done well together, their minds, emotions, and temperaments are at war—when He realizes all this—can you not see Him being sad?

If you have sex with someone you really and truly love before you're married, will that be held against you when God judges you about going to heaven?

God does not hold our past wrongdoings against us. In fact, just the opposite. "I will remember their sin [sexual or otherwise] no more" (Jeremiah 31:34). In fact, He gets rid of them so well that He casts them into the "depths of the sea" (Micah 7:19). When we recognize that our path has strayed from God's plan and decide from this point on to be on God's side, we are new persons in Christ Jesus. Now all that remains is for us to accept this gracious forgiveness and forgive ourselves.

I believe that one can be "spiritually revirginated." After forgiveness, in God's eyes, one can become a virgin again. Now, we will have to be ready for that sly old deceiver—our enemy—to try us on the same point again, for he knows where we are vulnerable. It may be even easier to fall the next time. Sex for some is a hard thing to forego once they have experienced it. For others, it has been such a bad experience under less than ideal circumstances that they never want to have anything to do with it again. Both are results which God hoped to shield us from. Think of God as "right there," trying to help you to keep your commitment to chastity, not eager to judge and zap you. He loves you and wants to be your best Helper, Supporter, and Comforter.

Situations Hard to Talk About

What do you do if your girlfriend is pregnant?

It only took ten words to ask that question, but what a world of implications! No one ever expects to have to face this situation, and I am sure you feel very bewildered.

First, make very sure that there is no question about the medical certainty of this. Just a late or missed period is not proof of pregnancy, although it is distressingly scary! Your county medical services will have facilities to make this test for her free, without reporting to anyone but her.

If you discover that your girlfriend is *not* pregnant, then you will have another opportunity to think over your sexual behavior and make decisions that protect you from this anxiety. No doubt you have already read that abstinence is the only perfect contraceptive! It has lots of other advantages too, and you will have time to think these through now.

If you discover that your girlfriend is pregnant, you will have some planning to do—together. Don't make another flawed decision to cop out and let her take care of things alone. Hang in there with your support for whatever choices the two of you make.

I would hope that both of you would feel able to tell your parents, for they can be very helpful at times like this. You may be saying, "You don't know *my* parents!" or "Her parents, they'd kill me/us!" That is what almost every young person in this situation believes. But actually, after the initial shock and disbelief, most parents come through as helpful and supportive. Be prepared, for shock and disappointment sometimes sound like anger. What it will all mean is that in their love and trust, it didn't occur to them that this could happen in their family.

TEENS HAVE QUESTIONS ABOUT THE "S" WORD 53

While you will want to listen to what they have to say and to the different suggestions that they may have, ultimately it will be up to your girlfriend and you to make the final decision. Your girlfriend's wishes should be considered first and foremost. It is her body, her life, which is so vitally involved. But whatever she decides, she will need much support, for there is no ideal solution to this problem. Very often a pastor, a physician, or a trusted Christian adult can also be involved. While such counselors used to think of marriage as the best solution, not all agree today that this is indicated. A poor marriage doesn't make a good background for any of the persons involved.

Whatever is decided, the best interests of the innocent little one should be carefully considered. That is more important than pride, embarrassment, or position. Never forget that God has met this problem many times. He has answers, and He will help you go through this and come out a wiser, more mature person. He won't let you down.

> **I had a boyfriend when I was sixteen, and I cared about him a lot. One day when he had something to drink, he raped me. It was the worst thing in the world. After that it seemed he didn't care as much, and it really hurt. It's been ___ years, and I am still not over it. What should I do?**

My heart just ached when I received this question, for it still showed so much hurt after a long time. It also demonstrated the harmful effects of even a little alcohol, probably taken thoughtlessly with no idea of the pain that it would be responsible for. Under the best of circumstances, we would like to think maybe his remorse and embarrassment made it hard for him to still be around. But we also have to allow that it was a thoughtless, uncaring act by someone thinking only of his own desires.

Being raped is one of the most terrible experiences that a woman can have. The results of it don't just go away with time. It can remain a continuing, haunting memory that can affect a person—emotionally and socially. I would urge you, and anyone who has also been raped, regardless of how long ago, to get counseling from someone who is reliable and experienced. Sometimes pastors, deans, or school counselors may be available. Part of the qualification of these trained people directs that whatever is told them in confidentiality cannot be repeated to anyone. You may want to ask your counselor if that is the way she or he operates, to assure yourself.

You need to be able to work through this bad experience so that you can begin to put it behind you and go on into the future without carrying this heavy burden with you. Please do this. *Please* do this. God bless.

> **I was just wondering, how are you supposed to feel if your cousin—whom you haven't seen in five years, then you finally do see him—makes a pass at you. Was I supposed to just let him make a pass at me? I always have no problems with any of my boyfriends, and then this happens. I felt so hurt. It happened during the summer, and it is still on my mind.**

This question points out the differences which sometimes exist between young men and women. While the young man involved may long since have forgotten what may have been a "routine" pass, the young lady is still bothered by it. She feels hurt and upset. She has every right to be upset. You see, something else is also involved here, and that is the relationship between the young woman and her cousin. We have laws in our country which prohibit marriage between close relatives, and in most states, that includes cousins. Sexual relationships would also seem to be inappropriate in these cases. In other words, there is an incest taboo against this kind of behavior. That is one of the reasons she feels so hurt about it. She should have been able to trust a cousin not to make aggressive moves on her. Families and relatives should be there to protect us, not to take advantage of us. You remember she said she could handle fellows who "make a pass," but something about this situation was dismaying.

I hope that if this should ever happen to you, your response will be a firm, loud: "STOP—you have no right to do

TEENS HAVE QUESTIONS ABOUT THE "S" WORD 55

this to me. From my cousin, as part of my family, I should be able to expect more respectful behavior." If he does not get the idea, enlist the help of someone else in the family who can be effective in helping him to understand his place.

Some people might say, "What's the big deal? You are making too much of it. He didn't actually do anything to you." But it *is* a big deal, and, yes, he *did* do something to you. He upset you not only for the moment but into the future. Good, clean, innocent fun does not make people feel uncomfortable, nor does it hurt their lives for months into the future.

I would give the same advice to this young woman as I did in the last question. Find some qualified, experienced counselor who can talk this over with you and help you put it behind you. Don't fail to do this.

> **How do you handle incest? I've been through it. Now I have a friend who's going through it, and it brings back all those feelings! Please answer. It's important!**

I wish I could say that this is not a very common question, but I cannot. Over and over again it is asked in questions much like this one. Far too many of our young girls, and some young boys, have been hurt in this traumatic way. It would be bad enough if the incident itself were all that was involved. But as this question illustrates, the pain can recur over and over again.

First I want to reassure you, that what happened to you when you were younger was *in no way your fault.* No one has the right to victimize you in this way. Often the person who inflicts this terrible act tries to implicate the child (of any age, including teens) in the blame. This is never true. It was a wrongful act committed against you, and you are not held in any way responsible. You are precious in God's sight, and He deplores what happened to you.

Even though at times you may feel that you have put this event behind you, it may continue to recur unless you get some professional help. Again I strongly urge you to find such a counselor. Perhaps a dean or a pastor can direct you to find the best possible resource. Please make this effort to begin dealing with this disabling memory so that you can plan for your future in a positive manner.

* * * * *

How much I have enjoyed going through these questions again! It reminds me of the original youth groups where they were first presented. These contacts with you have given me a firm impression that you are a solid group of fine young people who really want to be on the right track. I absolutely discount the labels sometimes given—"irresponsible, impulsive, unhearing." You have shown me a part of you that demands respect.

God sees you that way too, and loves you even more than we—your parents—can. He does not set standards for you to see how tough He can make it for you or to see you squirm. He knows you so well. He knows your peers so well. His greatest wish for you is your happiness, not just now while you are in your teens, but later when you become adults. Oh, how good He wants it to be for you when you marry! You can trust Him to know what is best for you now and always.

By the way, you may want to read on into the next section for unmarried adults. Maybe you have been thinking of some of these issues too.

Chapter 3

Unmarried Adults Are Asking

Our churches and neighborhoods have a larger number of unmarried adults than in the past. Some formerly marrieds have joined the single ranks again because they have lost a spouse through divorce or death. Many of these are trying to handle their lives while shouldering responsibilities for their children. Other singles have not yet married, and marriage for many is waiting longer and longer!

Several explanations exist. One is the length of time it takes now to prepare educationally for a career. Both women and men wish to further their prospects of a good future vocation. Add to this the many material things that now seem almost a necessity, and it can mean postponing marriage until it is possible to feel financially ready.

Many young people are aware of the escalating divorce rate. They note unhappy situations in their own homes and those of their peers. They have determined to take a long, careful look at marriage before they make a commitment. Some know firsthand the pain and disorganization that come with divorce. They want to avoid further trauma by waiting longer to make sure of their decisions. This certainly is not unreasonable.

However, another dilemma can follow this decision. What do singles do with the feelings of sexuality that are part of their personhood? They are bombarded from all directions with sexual stimuli—how should they handle these? The formerly accepted value of waiting till marriage to have sex has undergone tremendous weakening. People are saying, "I think times have changed, that virginity is an outdated expectation," or "How can you expect young people not to act upon God-given feelings?"

These questioners don't only include those without strong religious convictions. Some dedicated Christian young people want to think that premarital sex is morally acceptable behavior. Some have been sexual and feel guilty. Others do not. Some wish they could roll back the clock and erase part of their sexual history; others remain active.

The following questions demonstrate that young and older single adults are thinking carefully about these issues. I commend you for your thoughtful consideration of these sexual questions.

My boyfriend wants a text that forbids premarital sex. Is God really against it?

This is probably the most frequently asked question by those who are unmarried. So let's look at it and see if God indeed has given us guidelines for the sexual behavior of unmarried adults.

In Genesis 2:24 we have an opportunity to get some insights from the first marriage in Eden. God set down some guidelines here in advance that weren't intended to remedy a situation already in progress, but to provide a precedent for future sexual behaviors.

After God brought Adam to Eve, Adam said: "This is now bone of my bones and flesh of my flesh." The quotation marks end on Adam's speech, and God continues: "For this reason a man will leave his father and mother and be united with his wife and they will become one flesh." Even before there was a father and mother to leave, God wanted this new pair to understand that their relationship was to uniquely involve just the two of them. Then they were to experience a marriage covenant, a cleaving to one another. This reminded them that in this consummate union, vows of faithfulness were to be spoken. *After* these vows came the union of one-fleshness. In this union they felt no strangeness, no embarrassment, no shame. They felt as newlyweds can feel; blessed in this experience of sexual union.

But note again the sequence which God proclaimed right at the very beginning. First each leaves a past life to become part of a distinct and unique relationship. Then the couple shares a covenant and vows to one another their till-death-do-us-part commitment. Finally they celebrate their one-fleshness, the marital sexual embrace. I like to think that every intercourse experience between a husband and wife should be another opportunity to again act out these vows.

The book Song of Solomon also portrays this same sequence. Chapter 3:6-11 portrays the wedding procession on the day of the wedding. What follows encompasses the wedding ceremony proper. Only then is the Shulamite maiden addressed as Solomon's bride, after which she invites her groom to "partake of the fruits of her garden." Until then this has been a "locked garden," which denotes virginity.

Often unmarried people have felt that the seventh commandment does not speak to them, since they are not contemplating involvement with a married person. Careful biblical scholars realize that the seventh commandment, "Thou shalt not commit adultery," is understood to mean far more than illicit sex with a married person. It denotes every kind of unlawful sexual intercourse—premarital, extramarital, and postmarital. One theological dictionary says it this way: "It is an unconditional repudiation of all extra-marital and unnatural intercourse."

Neither does the New Testament leave doubt in our minds about the course that should be followed by the unmarried with regard to their sexuality. Acts records that the church council was giving thought to helping the new Gentile brethren realize their Christian responsibility. One of the things they were to abstain from was immorality—fornication, unchastity—the same behaviors we noted that were forbidden in the Old Testament. You can read about the whole incident in Acts 15.

Paul's prescription for "burning lust" was either to practice self-control—as he did—or to marry. Apparently there was no middle ground that allowed for gratification outside of marriage, no rationalization such as, "We are mature and can handle it," or "God understands our motive, and something that feels so right must *be* right for our relationship." No, Paul says it very plainly, sex is for married individuals only. He reiterates this in 1 Thessalonians 4:3-5 in these words: "It is God's will that you should be sanctified; that you should avoid sexual immorality, that each of you should learn to control his own body in a way that is holy and honorable, not in passionate lust like the heathen who do not know God." Concluding in verse 7: "For God did not call us to be impure, but to live a holy life." That seems quite clear, doesn't it?

Now, let's look at this from one other aspect. Is it right, then, to be virginal before marriage just because God "said so," or did God say so because He knows what is right (or true, reasonable, sound, flawless, perfect)? God knows what is right not only from a legalistic viewpoint, but also what is best for the children He knows so well, physically, emotionally, intellectually, and spiritually. In His wisdom, He seeks to protect His creatures from the confusion, the disorganization, and the pain that come from going against what is right. Not always immediately, mind you. In fact, the more immediate the sexual experience, the less likely two lovers are to see the difficult results that can come from this premarital behavior. But God's wisdom sees past the weeks and the years and to eternity. He wants what is best for us always.

Is it wrong to express one's feelings and emotions physically while still going out? If it is OK, how should I act?

In a relationship where there is no commitment or engagement, how much touching should be done?

How about veggie-sex (anything but intercourse)?

Here are three questions from three different countries. We can see that there is a general concern about how to act on emotions having to do with sexuality. Other questioners have put it even more bluntly, "How far can we go?"

To answer these questions, I would like to look with you at the whole sexual response pattern. This will provide information that we will need for the remainder of this book. It is only in the last thirty to thirty-five years that we have understood that there is a typical, orderly pattern to this part of our body functioning. Just as digestion, circulation, and respiration go through certain predictable, describable steps in the process

UNMARRIED ADULTS ARE ASKING

of carrying out their operations, so does sexuality. It is not a helter-skelter kind of experience that varies in everyone with no way to understand or regulate its conduct, as many have felt. Of course, we should have known better; God does not create haphazardly. He is a God of order. At least now we know what will happen when our bodies are stimulated sexually and what the undisturbed process will bring about.

Phase I: The Excitement Phase

This results from stimuli that have set in motion feelings of attraction, desire, and longing. For a woman, it may be incited by a sense of emotional closeness and a feeling of being cherished. It may be a look or a touch that makes her feel special and desirable. It may be something romantic like a favorite love song, a poem, a red rose, or a note. For a man it is more likely to be the sight of someone attractive, her movements, aroma, and touch. The excitement phase is evidenced in women by genital lubrication and in men by penile erection.

Phase II: The Plateau Phase

This phase is commonly referred to as foreplay. I do not like that term, however, since it seems to suggest that this is simply a prelude to the next, most important phase. I feel that this phase is such an important part of sexual response that unless it is given a special place in its own right, it gets lost in the urge to go on to the next phase. Some love relationships do not go past this love-play time, and that is appropriate for both men and women, even in marriage.

Some have referred to the purpose of this stage as providing a bonding between two people, which begins perhaps with simply a special, meaningful look or a light touch. From here there may be light kissing and touching of the face or head, then hugging and further expressions of love and tenderness. As the desire builds, probably the breasts will be touched next, and then the genitals may be caressed. As the tension mounts, the persons involved have a greater and stronger desire to unite their bodies until it is almost impossible to resist the intense urge for intercourse to take place. We will call this the love-play phase.

Phase III: The Orgasmic Phase

In this phase of climax, each experiences waves of pleasure and ecstatic gratification in her or his own way. This consummate experience, in its fullest physical and emotional intensity, is reserved for humans. I like to think of it as a special gift for a thinking, emoting creation. God could have decided upon a joyless, perfunctory intercourse experience engaged in only for procreation. But He did not. He designed that this act of one-fleshness should bring two committed persons together in a throb of unity. And with that delight, He also made it possible for them to experience the power of procreation.

Phase IV: The Resolution Phase

This phase ends the sequence. The body now returns slowly to its nonstimulated state. Heartbeat, respiration, and breathing all return to normal. Both partners feel an "afterglow"—a feeling of spentness and delight. In this most intimate of human experiences, a woman and a man feel as close as they ever will to the oneness that their marital state bestows.

Now, obviously, we are talking here about the ideal sexual responses. God's plan was that each couple should experience this pleasure. Unfortunately, since the emotional, physical, intellectual, and the social all would need to be perfect, too, one can see why there can be many problems between two lovers when imperfect conditions surround them.

Recalling this background, let's return to the questions asked. Our questioners want to know how much physical closeness is appropriate for Christians who believe that God has given clear instruction that the ultimate expression of sexuality is reserved for marriage. God Himself will have to tell us someday the many considerations He had in mind when He gave us these guidelines. But even with our finite understanding, we can realize that something so emotionally laden, so easily impaired by lack of understanding and commitment, must be protected. Too much pain has resulted from using this gift impulsively, carelessly, and ignorantly. So let's proceed on the basis that we accept God's wisdom in restricting sexual intercourse to marriage.

Looking at the phases, we note that the love-play (plateau)

phase goes directly into the orgasmic phase. Since such a fine line exists between the two phases, we realize that some parts of the love-play are going to belong to the marital bed. These behaviors would be the ones that bring about and go directly into immediate readiness for intercourse. Touching that does this would be questionable. The final phases of readying the vagina for penile insertion, through touching and caressing one another, would be involved. Many married lovers would testify that fondling the breasts would be the point where sexual intercourse was almost an undeniable desire. This type of touching, then, would be questionable. Can we say then that touching which causes a compelling need to continue to stimulate to orgasm is involved? That puts it pretty much up to some hard self-knowledge.

This point may not be the same for everyone. For some it is possible that even hugging and light kissing will cause tremendous urges which clamor for expression. Each person will have to examine his/her body feelings. Each person will have to know her/his own body well enough to know when he or she is getting near a desire for more than just enjoying being near and touching. We must each make a decision—not in the midst of the excitement of being together, but in the cool of the day where we can think it through carefully.

To some all of this may sound picky-picky, much ado about a little thing like a natural process. And young adults who have worked their way—sometimes virginally—through the teen years, may wonder if there should not be a different set of rules for them.

But many who have experienced the result of going against God's will in this matter, at any age, wish they could retrace their steps and reclaim their virginity. Emotional pain, disappointment, disillusion, feelings of having been used, loneliness after separation and rejection, change in life-plans, plunging self-esteem—all of these could be documented at length with case histories. God's shorthand way of protecting from all of these is simply, "If you trust Me to know what is best for you, you will follow My plan, regardless of your own inclinations."

What do you think of living together before marriage?

You have probably considered the divorce statistics, which only account for marriages that couples have given up on. Then you have no doubt added marriages that are just "toughing it out." It certainly explains why there is some reluctance on the part of some people to marry without some reassurance beforehand. Many of you want to know if your relationship can stand the test of day-to-day living stresses. You want to be sure you are suited to one another. It's difficult for some to faithfully accept God's plan for chastity till marriage in an age so far removed from the Garden of Eden and all its advantages.

That does not seem unreasonable—*except* that statistics reveal that living together before marriage does *not* help marriages to last longer or to have a better quality. In fact, the opposite seems to be the case. Dr. Neil Gennett of Yale University reports a study done with his associates which found that couples who live together prior to marriage had a divorce rate 80 percent higher than those who did not! Other studies, while not reporting the same high percentage, all agree that premarital living together does not help marriage. One study found that those who did *not* live together before their wedding had a more positive evaluation and higher adjustment score than those who did. It concluded that practice does *not* make perfect! Apparently a "lite" relationship—all the privileges and half the commitment—just does not pay off.

Some may ask, "Well, at least we can find out if we are sexually compatible." Not so! Even in the sexual area the studies showed at least as many problems. Nothing worked better.

Of itself, the physical act of intercourse is far less complicated than getting along on an emotional level. And emotional levels will deeply affect the physical. Prime areas that need to be explored which will deeply affect the emotional adjustment include: learning to communicate; learning to disagree and settle conflict; understanding one another's moods, needs, goals, and values; and working on intimacy dimensions. It does little good to know every square inch of

UNMARRIED ADULTS ARE ASKING

the partner's body and know only a small amount about what makes him or her tick on other levels.

Some have wondered, "How else will I know if my fiancé is going to be a responsive love partner?" Actually, it is easier to find out dressed than undressed! If she/he demonstrates concern for your feelings and is able to show appreciation, devotion, and sensitivity, those are good signs! If love can be verbally expressed, and if physical affection can be shown without always ending up in sexual demands or a sexual embrace, that's another good sign! One of the main complaints married women express is that they want more touching that doesn't always end up in bed. Furthermore, if two people have learned to talk things over without put-downs, withdrawals, and evasions, that is another excellent predictor. Relationships are more likely to be strengthened through emotional closeness than physical expertise.

I understand that sexuality is wonderful and that it is to be very much enjoyed within the commitment of marriage. However, we feel sexual before marriage, and these feelings are *strong*. What can we do . . .?

How about us that have been married before? This need is especially strong.

How can you break the habit of premarital intercourse? It is hard to stop!

Many single persons have strong sexual desires. This should not surprise us, since our culture consistently appeals to the sexual feelings people have. For some, the need for social and emotional intimacy is interpreted as sexual need, since we often attribute sexual feelings to any kind of touching. Ours is one of the few cultures that usually offers no more than a formal handshake in greeting. Too bad. This means that single persons could go days without a friendly touch.

Lonely people sometimes use sexual contact as an anesthetic to deaden their pain, for sex can give an illusion of caring. The feelings derived from sex are sometimes so powerful that they are mistaken for love. When it becomes evident that sex has not delivered love, the resultant disappointment and depression can be harder to cope with than the original loneliness. Being sexually active does not always deliver delight and satisfaction. Sometimes it pays off in remorse, a diminished self-concept, and more loneliness.

But that does not answer the question of how to deal with the urgency of sexual feelings. Here are some suggestions. First, be sure that what you are experiencing is not social loneliness and a need to feel important to someone. These conditions should be faced squarely and worked through so that they do not confuse the issue. Building new networks of friends, new activities, and new places can all contribute to relieving loneliness. Creative pursuits, physical fitness activities, volunteering—all these activities can provide profound satisfaction. They are not just poor seconds, either. Sometimes a therapist will have to encourage a married couple with inhibited sexual desire to spend *less* time in these pursuits and more in sexually stimulating activity precisely because these activities really *do* reduce sexual desire! Another added benefit that some of these activities can provide is touching, which can be experienced in working with the elderly, children, and others in need of appropriate hands-on nurturing.

It's important to discover what makes you most vulnerable to sexual feelings. Many discover that music, television, reading choices, suggestive conversations, or uninhibited daydreaming can be turn-ons. When on a diet, don't spend a lot of time in ice-cream parlors! Each person must be prepared for the strength and persistence of these feelings of desire. But you are in charge of your own thinking, which I think is good news!

Several questioners have asked directly about the practice of self-stimulation or masturbation as a means of reducing sexual tension. Masturbation is generally seen as a poor substitute for the warmth of another human being. It may also become a plainly lustful activity in which improper fantasies with masturbation can become obsessive to the point of withdrawal from meaningful social activity. In extreme cases, it can become an addiction.

The Bible does not speak specifically against this sexual activity, even though it does speak most clearly and specifi-

UNMARRIED ADULTS ARE ASKING

cally against many other sexual forms. We do know that the scriptural ideal for sexuality's expression is within a love relationship between a man and a woman, which is sanctioned in marriage. Persons contemplating an alternate means of expressing their sexuality will have to carefully consider their choice. (There is a question on masturbation in Chapter 1 that you may want to refer to.)

What difference does a piece of paper make, after all?

You are probably talking about the marriage certificate. Many pieces of paper make a *big* difference. If a university president decided to eliminate diplomas because they are only cheap pieces of paper, the student body would rise in indignation. A police officer failing to return a driver's license he had just checked—since it is such a small bit of paper—would be met with loud protest. Throughout our history, pieces of paper have assumed inestimable value.

A marriage certificate is a promise of commitment and fidelity that stands the test of time in a way that passionate words cannot. It stands for a commitment to work through problems, to stubbornly build, from tensions and conflicts, a strong, dependable union. This piece of paper indicates that, before God and other significant people, you have stated your intention to be faithful to your marriage vows. You have requested that legal powers acknowledge your commitment and you have invited God's church and His ministers to sanction, in a very special way, what you are promising to one another. Those are pretty substantial burdens to lay on a piece of paper, but very necessary ones.

If one who is single has fears and reservations about sex, how can he/she overcome this?

Enjoying our sexual feelings, wanting to be close, and looking forward to sexual consummation are very normal feelings. When a person recognizes that instead he or she feels reticence and even dread, something has interfered with what God intended. These negative emotions can result from bad messages from parents or others important to us. Lack of positive sex education can cause fear because of ignorance. Sometimes having had a bad experience as a child (which may not even be clearly recalled) can also interfere.

Extensive reading of Christian authors who help explain sexuality in a way that is altogether loving and desirable can sometimes change feelings. However, it may be necessary to talk to a therapist to help untangle the influences that are blocking normal feelings. Do not hesitate to do this. Many people have been helped to overcome these "handicaps," and go on to a fulfilling relationship.

How far can a single woman have a relationship with a married man and still feel safe so she doesn't become emotionally attached to him?

Any time a man or woman senses a growing interest in a married person of the opposite sex, it is a good time to stop, look, and listen. Many people in full-blown affairs state that at first they did not realize how much they were being drawn to that other person. The feeling was so gradual that it became overpowering before they were aware of its hold on them.

Married people who are not in a good relationship are more vulnerable than those who are happily married. Single persons who are active, contented, full of energy and enjoyment are in less jeopardy than those who feel lonely, unfulfilled, and unsure of their personal value.

When that other person becomes the object of a lot of thought and even daydreaming, when you look forward with great anticipation to seeing him or spending time where he is, when you feel you want to talk to her about things you don't want to discuss with anyone else, and when your greatest efforts to look attractive and appealing are directed to that person, then you need to take a hard look at what is going on and redirect yourself to safer channels. Affairs are not the glamorous "riding the crest" kinds of experiences for the most part. They appear this way sometimes, but those within them often characterize them as painful and defeating. Anything you can do to avoid the trauma that can engulf you and reach out to affect a whole family and network of friends should be done carefully and prayerfully.

UNMARRIED ADULTS ARE ASKING

Is premarital oral sex a sin?

Recalling our discussion of the four phases of sexual arousal, I believe that this type of sexual expression reaches right into the part of sexuality that belongs to marriage only. Sometimes couples use this activity to remain virginal, and still satisfy their desires. I cannot accept this. I believe that all behaviors which lead to a culmination of sexual stimulation belong in marriage and when practiced outside of this sacred bond are against God's plan for sexuality. (Oral-genital sexual expression will be discussed more fully in the next chapter.)

Is it forgivable? If a couple has participated in premarital sex often, but then realize it is wrong, and stop and ask forgiveness from God, can they still have a good marriage? Is there hope?

Oh, yes, indeed there is hope! Giving hope is what our God is best at! When a couple begins to treasure their relationship with their heavenly Father and seek to follow His will for their lives in this area, as in every other, God wants so much to give them happiness in their love for one another. Sometimes it seems harder for people to accept God's forgiveness for sexual sins than for other wrongdoing. Our culture tends to exalt this sin above all others in iniquity. Problems of guilt and remorse can affect a sexual relationship if the parties involved continue to cling to their guilt. But this will not be because God is continuing to afflict them with these feelings. He wants His beloved children to put all guilt behind them, accept His pardon, and grow in His love and approval.

How do a young man and his girlfriend know when they should get married?

What a good question! Far too often, young people have taken their feelings as the sole indicator that marriage is right for them. The overwhelming feelings of desire they experience when they are together are not in themselves an indication that marriage is right for them at this time.

Here are some better indicators: when they are at least

well on the road to being ready for their lifework; when they have many things in common such as religion, lifestyle choices, etc.; when they are beginning to recognize how to handle differences and have developed somewhat of a process for handling problems; when they realize that their level of dedication to God and the church is fairly equal; when they are able to discuss marriage with other responsible adults and then pray together for the right combination of all of these things. Does that sound like a pretty big order? Good! Marriage is a pretty big order. The more we can do to prepare for it, the better. Sometimes this includes waiting and working—yes, working—on the important issues. Premarital counseling will help with these steps and should be an absolute must for every couple considering marriage. If one or both of the parties involved resists going to a pastor or a marital counselor for this help, that in itself is an alarm of caution sounding! Go slow and insist!

What if I never get married? Does that mean I will never have sex in this world?

This question really troubles many young adults. That is understandable. Sexuality is a wonderful gift, and the inability to ever have this experience is seen as a deprivation. But having sex outside marriage is also a deprivation. A person will *still* never know the full joy of sexual love in its sanctioned atmosphere. When this love is not in the totality of a long-term, complete commitment, it will not bring full happiness. We are not talking here about short-term effects. We are talking long-term results, and no one knows more about long-term results than God does. He has suffered with us for thousands of years because of the results of choices made when people wanted their own way.

One lifetime is too short for us to experience everything. I have heard some people say that the biggest thrill of their lives was an ovation following the conducting of an oratorio or soloing before a large, appreciative audience. Most of us will never know that thrill. A Nobel Prize winner would tell us that nothing compares to the elation he feels when his name is publicly announced and he travels to receive his reward. A big-league ballplayer experiences a very rare and special thrill when his home run wins the World Series. There are many grand and wonderful experiences that many of us won't know firsthand. But one of the things God wanted us to *keep* from experiencing is that pain which often results from rejecting His guidelines for our sexuality. Which brings us to the next question.

Will there be marriage and sex in heaven?

This is a critical question for some people. If they could be sure there will be marriage and sex in heaven, it wouldn't seem so urgent to have it here on earth! In fact, some people have told me they actually pray for the Lord to delay His coming until they have had a chance at this fulfillment on earth! God really must be perplexed by this prayer, for it seems to be saying that He has run out of creative ideas and can't make heaven even as good as He did this earth! Yet we are told that we can't even dream up anything as wonderful as what He has already planned for us—and that's not just golden streets and unfading flowers.

Families were God's idea in the first place. The first family was the heavenly family (Paul speaks about the families on earth and heaven in Ephesians 3:14-16). The first major problem was in the heavenly family. But God didn't give up on families. He again introduced them into His earthly plan, but it hasn't been perfect here either. However, I believe that God will not give up on His plan for families in the new earth anymore than He gave up on His plan for families in our present world.

God will not take something away from us and substitute something inferior in its place. I think He has something far superior to what we now enjoy as we interact with our wives and husbands, and that it will include them. I can just imagine someone saying in heaven, "And to think that we wanted God to postpone this glorious existence for those damaged, often broken, painful relationships!" It's like being reluctant to trade in a beat-up, small compact car for a Rolls-Royce or a Ferrari. Even that is a feeble illustration. Trust Him! He knows what makes people happiest.

Can you suggest ways to relate positively to a homosexual or lesbian in the family or in the church?

I have received several questions relating to homosexuality. People ask what causes it, why people do it, and if homosexuals are different from other people. There seems to be a great deal of curiosity and, at the same time, confusion as to how to relate to people who are homosexual, whether male or female.

Unfortunately, as Christians, we do not have a good track record relating to people we consider different. We are too often judgmental and thoughtless. Some homosexuals have even been asked to leave a Seventh-day Adventist church and to refrain from worshiping with their congregation. Some have been thrown out of their homes. Many folk feel that homosexuals deliberately and arbitrarily decide for this sexual orientation. Others feel that it would be a simple matter of redirecting one's sexual desires to become heterosexual.

Heterosexuals need to realize that it would be just as difficult to ask a homosexual to change a preference as it would to demand that a heterosexual person become homosexual. No, we do not know why some people are homosexual and some heterosexual. Evidence suggests that it could very well be biological. For this reason, I believe that Christians who profess hatred, aversion, and revulsion against their homosexual sisters and brothers need to rethink their position.

Rather than demonstrating rejection and separation, we should offer understanding, accepting them as human beings just as worthy of God's love as we are. Our churches are not meant to be exclusive clubs for those who consider themselves whole persons, but communities to minister to all of His family.

I am a single mother with a little boy to raise. How can I give him a positive feeling about marriage and sexuality when I don't feel that way myself?

Bless you for realizing the need to help your little boy to see sexuality and marriage in the right light. Whatever cir-

UNMARRIED ADULTS ARE ASKING

cumstances brought about these feelings, they are shared by many other women (and men). Our churches are now beginning to realize the value of providing some education, support, and nurture for single parents. Churches are planning seminars, church workshops, and social events to meet this need. If your church has not yet taken this approach, talk to your pastor and his wife and to other church officers. See what can be started. At the very least, those of you who are single parents can get together in a group for study and discussion groups. The Family Life Ministries at the General Conference has workbook material which would be helpful, along with bibliographies that will serve as resource materials for your group discussions.

More than this, each church member should realize that your little son is also part of their own church family. You need more than assurance of prayers—you need tangible help. This may consist of an offer of baby-sitting for a couple of hours now and then so you can do your shopping or go jogging. It should also include invitations for home meals, picnics, and outings. This will give your little boy an opportunity to see dads operating within families, and wholesome interaction between wives and husbands.

Let me say one more thing to you. Please do not involve your little son in hearing negative, critical remarks about his father. He will be greatly handicapped by feeling that his dad is one of the bad guys! Keep as positive as you can about that half of his gene inheritance. In the long run, you will not come out looking better when you criticize his dad, however subtly. This may be very hard for you, as it is for others. I came from a home that was dysfunctional and finally broken. But the greatest gift both my mother and father gave me was never to speak unkindly or critically about the other. I admire and applaud them for that. So will your son someday.

Chapter 4

Beyond the "I Do's"

Have you read the wonderful instruction in Deuteronomy 24:5? It's just right for newlyweds! Listen, "If a man has recently married, he must not be sent to war or have any other duty [this can be interpreted as business or public service as well] laid on him. For one year he is to be free to stay home and bring happiness to the wife he has married" (NIV). Now, that is some great plan! Think of all the adjustments that could be worked through without rushing, intrusions, interferences, or deadlines. I am not sure how the economy would fare, but I am sure that it must have worked well enough then and probably paid dividends in happier, longer-lasting relationships.

One of the adjustments that newly-marrieds face is the sexual aspect of their interaction. Having been sexually active with one another in advance of marriage is no advantage, as we found in the last chapter. Having been sexually active with other persons may actually be a detriment. Being virginal is no guarantee that everything is going to be instantly perfect, either.

How, then, can a couple ensure a good physical relationship? I like to think of the base of their sexuality as having three supports. None alone is sufficient. Even having two of these three will not be sufficient. All are necessary. These are *attitude*, *knowledge*, and *commitment*. If couples have received consistently positive messages about the sexual experience, and they feel optimistic and eager to enter into this relationship with no unreal expectations, that will give them an A in *attitude*! Unfortunately, it is very difficult, if not impossible, to get through our culture without sexuality having been misrepresented somehow. This means that many people will have some nagging feelings or questions and attitudes that may be reawakened when there are deficits in the other areas.

Knowledge about the physical expression of their love includes knowing about the specifics of anatomy and physiology of female and male, the sexual response pattern, and what each can do to promote a good experience not only for oneself, but for the other. This knowledge would instruct about those most important, even *crucial*, emotional components that can make or break good sex. If the personal interaction does not include feelings of being cherished and respected by the other, their physical union could be sabotaged.

The other ingredient, *commitment*, recognizes that it's nearly impossible to be perfectly prepared in the other two aspects. But because they have pledged their undying love to one another, they are committed to doing whatever is necessary to work through their misunderstandings and differences, and to bring about the best possible sexual experience for each of them.

The following questions clue us in to the realization that many problem areas exist, as well as questions about married sexuality. Most of the ones we are going to answer in this chapter come from young marrieds. Here is what they are asking.

Problems About Sexual Expression

What would you say is the part that sexual intercourse plays in marriage?

I believe that intercourse plays a bonding role in marriage. The one-fleshness that distinguishes sexual intercourse connotes nearness, closeness, warmth, and acceptance. We might call all of these important components of intimacy, without which marriage cannot flourish. (Understand that sexual intercourse is not the only component of intimacy. But it does enhance a relationship that two people have exclusively with one another, which makes it the more special.) I believe this is one of the reasons why God gave to sexual intercourse the elements of delight, pleasure—and yes, ecstasy.

God could have created us to fulfill His "be fruitful and multiply" mandate without sensing any pleasure in the process. It could have been a strictly biological experience, engaged in only at times when children were planned. But God did not do that. He made us persons with the capability of enjoying the sexual experience, whether for procreation or for pure pleasure. We cannot read Song of Solomon without realizing what a surprisingly joyous experience God intended a man and a woman to have through their sexuality. When we seek the pleasure that God intended us to experience, we continue to feel a closeness, a union with our spouses which can take us through the ups and downs of everyday living. We can feel cherished and loved in a world that sometimes makes it tough to retain those feelings.

Healthwise, how often should a couple have sexual intercourse within a week?

No average or norm exists; neither is there a health standard for frequency of intercourse. For some couples, daily expression may be prized by both. Others might be perfectly satisfied with sex every week or so. Often men prefer sex more frequently, and women generally are satisfied with less. But this is not always the case; for some couples it is the reverse. This isn't saying that one is wrong and the other right. Ages, temperaments, and background messages about sexuality are important factors. The amount of satisfaction each derives when they are together is also a factor. Some couples have different levels of sexual desire. After some time, couples usually come to a compromise, and each can be satisfied. However, the *way* they handle this compromise *can* cause problems. If frequency of intercourse becomes a source of conflict, if they punish one another by withholding, and if they are not able to discuss their differences without angry outbursts and/or withdrawal, then the problem may not be as much with sexuality as in their way of relating to one another.

My partner and I have different ideas . . . does negotiating our "love play" destroy its spontaneity and integrity?

My first impulse was to say quickly, "No, talking things over and coming to a compromise does *not* destroy love play's spontaneity!" Then I paused to realize that what one person calls negotiating, another might call dictating or demanding. So let me put it this way: If a wife and husband enter into a loving discussion in which each gets to say what she/he wishes to say without defensiveness or interruption, then it could be helpful. If the goal is not to get one's way, but to enhance their love play, great! *Spontaneity* is a somewhat overworked word in the area of sexuality anyway. Sometimes we tend to regard spur-of-the-moment, unplanned, "carried away" sex as superior to that which has been talked about and planned. Actually, the latter can sometimes even be more pleasurable, for it gives us the opportunity to enjoy the anticipation of things to come. All the best restaurants and concerts insist on prior planning and reservations, and that does not take away the pleasure of these events. It only gives time to anticipate with delight.

What can I do about my husband, when even though he loves me, he just cannot express it? He can't even reach and touch or be touched.

As I am looking at this, I wonder if your husband is not like many other men with this problem. They realize their "inability" and would give just about anything to be verbally demonstrative. You say he loves you. He probably would like nothing better than to be just the kind of lover you want him to be. Most men really want to be good lovers. But his background makes it terribly difficult for him to be open and expressive.

One way will *not* help, and that is constantly bringing it up and berating him for being this way and not meeting your needs. The more he senses you are dissatisfied and disapproving, the more immobilized he may become. Since it is a well-known axiom that you can't change anyone but yourself, let us start there and forget about trying to change him. Maybe in your disappointment—and even impatience—you have also stopped being expressive and demonstrative. Perhaps you will have to start by doing for him just exactly what you wish he would do for you.

When he does something particularly loving, like bringing

home the paycheck or washing the car (yes, sometimes this is how men express their love), tell him that you are experiencing it as his love words. Then you could be lighthearted about it and say jokingly, "Now if I could just hear it out loud, we would have it made!" Then leave the subject. Don't belabor it. Men really dislike the way we women sometimes are unable to leave a thing alone once it is said. If it is difficult for him to be verbal, don't make an extra demand on him by waiting around to see how he will respond to the latest hint.

These changes in you could bring about eventual changes in him. But aside from that, it will make you a happier, more contented person just to know that you are maturing in the relationship.

We hope that your church is among those with marriage enrichment opportunities, where couples can sometimes learn more about their communication patterns. If his reluctance to touch or be touched is deep-seated, it may be that talking with a therapist could help the two of you cope with this situation together.

How do you relate to your husband that sex doesn't *start* in the bedroom?

Here it is! The most frequently asked question of all! If women could get this one point across to husbands everywhere, we would enhance the sexual response of our gender immeasurably. Women want times of loving, kissing, and hugging that have nothing to do with intercourse. Being treated matter-of-factly and even coldly during the day does not prepare for good sex that night. Being loving, caring, and demonstrative all day does. This should not be a toilsome task for a lover—which most men want to be.

I have had women tell me that they sometimes repulse and respond coldly to a certain kind of touching because they know what it is leading up to—sex! "Pecks on the cheek may be harmless," one woman said, "but watch out for the prolonged one on the lips or even the one on the back of the neck!" Other women say that they are careful not to be too loving themselves, because their husbands translate that into asking for sex! What a loss of love nourishment because every loving demonstration turns out to be a direct path to intercourse.

"Well, what are kissing and hugging for anyway if they're not for making love?" one man asked. Here's what women answer. "Hugging, kissing, and touching were fun before we were married, even when we both had the goal of waiting till marriage for total sexuality. It felt good to be chosen for special demonstrations of affection. No one had to tell us to hug and kiss for a while before we came home from our dates—that came easily! So why is it not seen as a delightful addition to our loving repertoire now that we are married?" Women want to feel loved and desirable all day, not just in the bedroom!

Our bodies were made to respond to tenderness and touching all over, not just genitally. Sometimes in marriage the genital is emphasized, and other touching is retired. The word, then, gentlemen, is: good lovers hug, kiss, cuddle, caress, snuggle, and lovingly touch many times during the day when intercourse is not even thought of. Your wives will be much more responsive when you follow this program!

My wife says her family did not show affection when she was growing up; therefore, this gives her a license to be unaffectionate. She states that I need to learn to accept her for herself.

This question shows the opposite side of the coin from the last one. Here a husband feels that his wife does not return his desire to be affectionate. The wife believes her husband should meet her where she is, but she does not seem to realize that he would also like her to accept his needs as valid. Perhaps this is another situation where she doesn't know how to allow herself to be open and demonstrative. She has had no models. She may have been given so many prohibitions about touching when she was a teenager that she finds it hard now to change the script. The sad part is that she is not only denying her husband the pleasures of closeness, she is missing something that both wives and husbands can appreciate.

Sometimes women might feel that they need to control the sexuality in their lives, or else it might get out of hand! But a love relationship between a wife and husband cannot continue without demonstrations of affection. We all have traits in our makeup that are the result of heredity or environment. Sometimes we need to think about how we can alter these rather than harm our relationship. None of us were reared in such a perfect atmosphere that we have come through without some nicks and scars in our personalities. But when we love someone, our desire is to be as careful with their feelings as we want them to be with our own.

Berating, begging, or scolding his wife will not help a man bring about what he desires. He can only change himself and hope that these changes will affect her. Maybe they could talk together about what he does that makes her feel most loved. Then he can share his ideas on that. Together they should read the great love stories of the Bible. Song of Solomon describes specific love demonstrations between a husband and wife. Spend time with this book, reading it together—out loud. The woman in this love story makes more advances and expresses her love more often than the groom does, and that says something that many women need to pay attention to.

If a man does not get the benefits he feels he should before going to sleep, could that cause him to "hog" the covers? Maybe to get the last word?

Are you smiling at this question as I did when I first read it? Another woman says that her husband "punishes" her when she won't have sex with him. These incidents demonstrate how closely the sexual interaction can be related to other parts of our thinking. Perhaps both husbands would be shocked if they thought their wives felt that their actions were deliberate.

What I see here is the need for a little discussion on the marital ethics of initiation and refusal. First, let me say that many women *do* have a way of rejecting a sexual suggestion that is in itself inciting. "Not again!" or "Is that all you ever think of?" or other similar comments do not bring on a good feeling in any man. It sounds like a personal rejection, and since it is also a sexual refusal, it is the ultimate put-down. Never mind that it shouldn't be, it is. Our culture has taught our husbands, through no fault of their own, that sex and love are the same. No sex means no love. Furthermore, when sexual overtures are refused crudely and thoughtlessly, a wife can wipe out her husband's feeling of effective maleness.

How much better for her to say something like, "I'm so glad you find me desirable/attractive/sexy. I wish I felt that way tonight. But it's been a tough day, and I am really tired/preoccupied/worried/wiped out. Could we postpone our lovemaking till tomorrow night [or another *specific* time—not infinity!]?" Now, instead of a rejection, we have a loving postponement.

If she doesn't follow through and is consistently unavailable for lovemaking, she should ask herself, why. He will certainly wonder! He may want to explore his initiation process. Maybe she doesn't like to be grabbed and *mauled* (a word frequently used by disappointed wives) without the least attention paid to wooing, verbally affirming, and bonding. Perhaps you will both have to decide that enough is at stake here to talk to a therapist to see what is causing "getting together" problems.

You will note I used the word *bonding* a few lines earlier. This concept refers to the stages that a couple generally go through to proceed from the significant look, the first touch, the initiating kiss, to intercourse itself. This should not be a goal-oriented journey. It should consist of kissing and touching, which gradually become more intense. These are interspersed with love dialogue and sometimes simply lying back in one another's arms and relaxing before further caressing takes place. Women usually react negatively to lovemaking that goes from A to Z with mechanical precision. Sometimes this lovemaking bypasses F to X completely. Bonding brings a couple closer together and brings them gradually to uniting of not only bodies, but souls and, yes, spirits.

Should a woman be honest with her partner about what she doesn't like about his lovemaking? Or is she supposed to suffer and never say anything because wives have this obligation to their husbands?

I am always a little wary when I tell wives and husbands to be honest with one another. There are two opposite kinds of honesty. There is the brutal, uncaring honesty. Example: "You are a terrible lover, and I dread having sex with you." Then there is loving honesty. Example: "I really want to have a good sexual relationship with you. I am glad you love me, and I want to tell you some of the things we might both do to make our lovemaking special for each of us."

I am not suggesting that this will be the end of all of your problems. But it can be a beginning. Bad patterns of behavior are not easily and quickly righted. It may take several of these "loving honesty" exchanges to get his attention. But as Paul reminds us, love is patient and kind and doesn't keep score. Look at this as a growth experience that will show in your interaction with your children and others in your life.

No, a woman is not supposed to "suffer and never say anything." She is not obligated to allow him to make her miserable. He is obligated to bring her happiness. *Both* husbands and wives are responsible to one another to bring health to their marriage and joy to their marriage bed.

Is there a wrong kind of sex for a couple to have?

Yes, I believe there is. Any sexual behavior that treats one or the other on an animalistic level is "wrong." Now, what do I mean by that? This term is used by many authors, and speaks about any relationship that is thoughtless, irresponsible, self-serving, noncommitted, and lacks tenderness. This kind of a sexual relationship erodes love and causes trauma and conflict.

This kind of a sexual relationship also says wrong things about God's love. His love is often depicted in marital/sexual terminology. Our love for one another should take as its model His great love for His bride. Sometimes we don't make that look so good!

What about oral sex? Is it appropriate for Christians?

Questions on oral-genital sexual stimulation are among those that I am most frequently asked. Sincere Christian

BEYOND THE "I DO'S"

husbands and wives want to know if this is an acceptable part of their love repertoire. Since the Bible is so forthright about the sexual things it disapproves of, they wonder why no instruction is given about what is proper in the area of lovemaking in marriage.

First, let us distinguish between oral-genital sexual stimulation as part of the love play that leads directly to sexual intercourse and the exclusive use of oral-genital stimulation, which takes the place of intercourse. This latter is sometimes used by unmarried (or married) couples to prevent pregnancy. Sometimes unmarried young persons make love in this manner to preserve the illusion that they are still virginal.

Most Christian thinkers who have written on this topic feel more comfortable with oral-genital stimulation as a prelude to intercourse. There is something so special about the face-to-face "knowing" of a wife and husband. Only humans are gifted with this special capacity. To complete the picture, we should recognize that in some cases where it is not medically possible for one or the other to enjoy climax in lovemaking without oral stimulation, couples have this means of satisfaction.

Where we have no biblical instruction or other definitive counsel, I believe that we should be careful in setting guidelines which suit our own biases. For some couples, using their lips to kiss and caress the entire body of their beloved can be a joyous experience—this part of their interaction expresses for them an all-encompassing love. For others, or for one or the other of the couple, it is possible that feelings of repulsion by the genital area, or at least oral contact with it, cannot be overcome. I believe that this decision should be honored by either spouse.

I would be very concerned if one spouse was trying to force this type of love play on an unwilling partner. Sometimes it becomes almost an obsession for one partner or the other to initiate this variation. I believe that preoccupation with this demand—or any other, for that matter—says something negative about the whole relationship, not simply the sexual aspect. Each spouse should be willing to discuss this questions with openness, respect a decision made with equanimity and in good grace, and happily continue lovemaking in ways each can joyously accept.

Do worry and insecurity block one's ability to get aroused for sex?

You're right. They certainly do. So do fatigue, preoccupation with work/children/recreation, and boredom. In fact so many of these things now operate in our culture that often people experience a lack of desire for sexual activity, and many of those are young people. It is not an exclusively middle-age or retirement phenomenon. Again this demonstrates the clear tie-in between sexuality and all the other parts of our being. It also helps us recognize the special regard this precious experience deserves. We should not let it get pushed aside, consistently, for any of these reasons.

Is it right to have sex on Friday night or on the Sabbath day?

Centuries ago, anything sexual was seen by the church in power as depraved and degraded, and to be avoided except for procreation. It's easy to understand why people felt that it was wrong to enjoy something so questionable on the holy hours of the Sabbath. However, we hope that few in our Christian community see sex in that negative light now. We recognize that sexuality is the highest form of human communication between a husband and wife. It is God's plan for them to share this one-fleshness, bonding them in a faithful relationship. That puts a different light on this old prohibition. Sometimes the message in Isaiah 58:13, which asks His children not to do their "own pleasure" (or as the NIV states, "doing as you please on my holy day"), is interpreted as saying that we should not enjoy the pleasures of lovemaking on Sabbath. If we followed this interpretation as stated, we would have to quit eating, fellowshiping, singing, and even going to church—if church is as pleasurable for you as it is for me! Careful scholars tell us that this verse tries to help people see that they shouldn't go about the same old activities and business tasks as they do on every other day.

In some Jewish writings, ancient Hebrews were instructed to be ready for the Sabbath an hour before sundown. Then, in preparation for the Sabbath, they were to read the Song of Solomon. In preparation for this celebration, they were to turn their thoughts not only to their own love, but to rejoice in God's love for His bride, the community of believers.

When this human love takes for its model the lovers of this biblical Song of Songs, what could be more appropriate? When delight, commitment, and grateful joyousness are expressed, what a bond between the Creator and His creatures! But when insensitivity, grudging compliance, and attention to only body needs are foremost, it is not an activity which the Sabbath, or any other day, could bless.

If I don't have sex often, is there something wrong with me?

Sexual desire varies a great deal in individuals. More important than how often you want sex is how this matches up with your spouse's desires. When there is a great discrepancy here, it can be a problem. When a marriage is working well, and there is love, consideration, and good communication between the partners, they usually come to a resolution. This means that one person will have sex a little more often than he or she might like, and the other a little less often.

Sometimes a woman may not feel desirous when her husband does, but she will accept lovemaking as an expression of her love for him. Whether she is orgasmic or not may be immaterial. She can still be a sexual partner. At another time, the wife may be seriously interested in an orgasmic experience but her husband, for one reason or another, may not readily experience an erection. He can still fill her needs by caressing the parts of her body that arouse her sexually and lead to orgasm. Both can then feel satisfied that they have experienced lovemaking. Sometimes after couples have experienced the many good feelings that come from nonintercourse activities—cuddling, hugging, caressing, kissing with a loving verbal commentary, they find that this meets some of their sexual needs. Often what the couple really wants is closeness, and one or both think this can only be achieved through intercourse. Enlarging their repertoire of loving can help them truly appreciate the non-intercourse aspects of love play.

If your question means that you don't like sex at all and want to have it as little as possible, then we are talking about something else than different levels of sexual arousal and desire. We have already mentioned many things that can interfere with sexual arousal and desire. The problem could be emotional, physical, situational (under some circumstances you enjoy it—say on a weekend trip together or after an evening of sharing and closeness), or because neither one of you has discussed how best you can enjoy one another's lovemaking. You may not have the type of stimulation you need to be aroused. If any of these situations sound familiar to you, don't spend the rest of your life not wanting to have sex. Being sexually aroused is a normal body function. Find out what is standing in the way of your body responding the way it was meant to.

Seeing that men have the responsibility to earn and financially prepare and adequately provide that lovely home, should wives not be taught that he's earned her total consideration for his fulfillment, even if at times she's not completely excited?

Let's see how this question sounds another way. "Seeing that women have the responsibility to cook, clean, scrub, launder, iron, take care of children, sometimes help with paying the bills, keeping track of the insurance, taking the clothes to the cleaners—shouldn't husbands be taught that she has earned his total consideration for her needs always to be met, even when at times he doesn't want to?"

But I don't like to think of making love as being a return for favors, be it either man or woman. Sexual communication is neither a reward nor a punishment. It is a demonstration of caring that results from feelings of being cherished, appreciated, and wooed. No one has ever been able to show that working to *support* a family is harder than working to *take care* of one in the home. And believe me, some have tried to prove that—and were shocked at the never-ending tasks of housekeeping. Simply put, men could not do without women in the home any more than women could do without men.

Sexuality is never at its best where there is conflict, competition, or power plays. Paul's 1 Corinthians list of the components of love can apply to sexual love just as it does to any other kind of love. Sexual love would then be seen as patient, kind, not envious, not proud, not rude, not self-seeking, not easily angered, and a love that keeps no record of grievances. Now there is a prescription for sexual love that would make lives truly edenically happy! I can guarantee you without a doubt, that it will work much better than demanding rights!

Is it abnormal for a woman not to reach a climax every time she has sex with her partner?

No, this is not at all unusual. In fact, only a small percentage of women reach orgasm every single time they make love. We have already touched on some of these reasons. Fatigue, worry, illness, emotional stress, and problems in the interpersonal relationship are a few things that can affect a sexual experience. But even if all these things were cleared up, a woman is just more responsive at some times than at others. The wife or her husband should not expect her to be orgasmic every time she has intercourse. Orgasm is only one part of the lovemaking sequence. Sometimes it can be overemphasized. It is much better to think in terms of experiencing and enjoying the good feelings that touching the total body provide, and quit trying to live up to some impossible goal.

How can you reconcile an early morning person with a night person so that you can have time for intimacy? We rarely go to bed together, and my wife spends a lot of time with the children at night in their bedrooms. Night seems to be the best time to talk for me.

Each of you will probably have to make some adjustments. Maybe if you were to help her with bathing the children, reading the stories, and talking with each of them before they go to bed, this would release some of her time. Some women resent being the only ones involved in bedtime activities. That takes away a lot of the desire to be involved in intimacy with an otherwise uninvolved husband. Since your children would be benefited by interaction with both of you, they would receive side benefits too.

Going to bed together at night is a great time for intimacy. You may have already guessed that I am not talking only of sexual intimacy. Talking together, recounting the day, and offering words of validation and support are all parts of an intimate relationship. When one spouse wishes to stay up longer to take care of other duties, I suggest that the couple spend a few minutes lying on the bed when the early-to-bed person gets ready to turn in. Then the later-to-bed person can get back up and read, pursue a hobby, or work.

To accommodate that late-to-bedder, the other spouse can make a point of staying up later a night or two to spend time together. Intimacy does not take care of itself. It must be planned and nourished. It is the responsibility of both wife and husband. Each needs to cherish this closeness by altering behaviors that have a tendency to starve it.

Problems That Can Be Troublesome

How can I learn to like sex? Due to pornography and rape I don't.

I am always saddened by the far-too-frequent references to violent sexual experiences that women have had. Any woman who in the past has been exposed to rape, incest, or any other type of sexual abuse has my deepest sympathy. But that is not enough. I believe that you also need some professional help through counseling. These horrendous traumas have a predictable tendency to affect the way you—or any other woman in your situation—feels about sex, even many years later. Your feelings springing from revulsion and aversion must be dealt with. Simply repeating the incident to another nonprofessional friend is usually not enough. I urge you, and others in your situation, to find help and work through this problem.

Since pornography is so many times directed to the very

thing you went through, it is not surprising that it affects you. Many women without your sad history loathe it as well. It never presents sexuality in a lovely way. They couldn't find such a good market for it if it did! The whole act of sex, and women—as well as men—are degraded and made to be objects and victims, instead of loving partners. My greatest rage is directed against kiddie porn, which makes children the innocent victims of lust and greed.

If we want our homes to reflect the philosophy that sex is God-given, that it is hedged about by His special protective safeguards as something altogether pure and lovely, pornography will have no place in our homes or in our thinking.

When this type of reading has become an addiction for a person, he or she might want to get some help to find out why it has such a strong attraction.

What will be your counsel to a new married couple who did not know how to have sex, since both were virgins when they got married?

My first thought was: how wonderful that you will both begin your sexual love with no leftovers! You see, I receive questions that ask what can be done with memories that one has of former sexual experiences, either from another marriage or premaritally. (See next question.) You will have nothing of this nature to threaten your sexual relationship.

Excellent Christian sex manuals are now available from Christian bookstores. Find several of these and read them out loud together. No prescribed schedule exists for when you should be ready to consummate your marriage. But if you find yourselves continuing to postpone this union because of fear and uncertainty, you may want to consider getting some counsel. It may be that other things from the past are affecting one or the other of you, making you reluctant. This may need to be explored.

What can I do with flashbacks of past sex before marriage?

Your question demonstrates one of the good reasons to contain sex within the protected marriage parameters. Comparisons can affect current sexual experience. Since you and you alone can control the material that you give conscious thought to, you *can* will yourself to change mental pictures that insinuate themselves upon your thinking. You cannot control the initial stimuli, but you can refuse to continue to think about these past situations.

Give them to your heavenly Counselor. He does not want these thoughts to be a problem to you now. He is not saying, "See, I told you to be chaste—see what happened!" No. That is not God's way. He desires to work with you to dim these pictures and alleviate your memory of them. Your responsibility will be to *will* to change those thoughts—immediately! Far too often one can play around with them and almost nourish them by leaving them in the mind. A quick, determined, and loud inner STOP can do wonders in relieving this problem over time. God is anxiously waiting to be your partner in this venture!

My husband has problems with premature ejaculation. Can anything be done? I don't experience orgasm when my husband makes love to me, since we can't engage in much love play.

Yes, something can be done about this situation, and it usually works very well. A sex counselor can help you with this learning experience and would want both of you to be present. The problem affects both of you, and both will need to be involved in the solution. Look for a therapist who is accredited by the American Association of Sex Educators, Counselors, and Therapists (AASECT, for short). It is usually not a long, drawn-out therapy and can bring good results which both of you will be helped by.

When sexual play does not last long enough for you to have sufficient stimulation for orgasm, that is only part of it. As it is now, neither of you enjoys those wonderful, important parts of lovemaking. You are both getting short-changed!

Your husband might feel better about seeking therapy if he realized that this is a common problem, particularly among younger men. This, of course, doesn't exclude older men from being affected too. Since this is the most easily helped among

BEYOND THE "I DO'S"

sexual problems, it's a shame to have years of frustration accumulating. It takes courage to make a decision for counseling, but it's worth it.

> **We have been married for __ years and have several fine children. This is my wife's first marriage, but my second. She feels that we should never have been married because of the divorce circumstance. Now any problem is seen as God's punishment on our marriage.**

How sad for all of you! However, hear the good news. God's blessings are not limited by ideal circumstances. If this were so, we would *all* be doomed. Better still is the news that God can take a past event in our lives that was against His will and make good come from it. He does not continuously and repeatedly punish us for sins in the past. He takes us right where we are and relieves us of guilt and remorse, setting us up on "higher ground."

Bad things can happen to good people too. That is the nature of the world we live in. But His omniscience can make good things spring from those bad things. God wants your home to be happy and full of love, now. He wants your little ones to feel an atmosphere of caring and approval, not just between them and their parents, but between their parents as well.

Both of you would be helped by reading together some materials on forgiveness. Your pastor or your closest Christian bookstore would be able to direct you to fine resources. Don't delay! Through your constant love and reassurance, your wife can be helped to put behind her the things that God wishes her to "remember no more." He has already forgotten. (Meanwhile, read Jeremiah 31:34, Micah 7:10, and Psalm 103:12.)

> **Sometimes the "after baby" blues decrease and a wife's sexuality can be helped if the man will agree to take the night shift with the baby. He would respond to the night change of diapers or take a small child to the bathroom at 2:00 a.m. [or**

walk a crying, colicky infant!]. It seems like a little thing, but it says "I love you" and shows it too.

This remark is obviously by a woman who has been there! (I will have to admit to personally adding the part about the colicky baby—based on memories of my own and the appreciation due a helping husband!) Many husbands have remarked that a new baby puts sex into long hibernation for them, and they sometimes say it with resentment. Here we have a response for them. I know it's valid, for many women have echoed the sentiments expressed above. Fatigue and a heightened sense of twenty-four-hour responsibility can wear away sexual desire. But here is a way to help and awaken sexual response. I should add here, however, that sometimes it *is* possible for a mother to become overinvolved with her baby to the point of forgetting what the primary love relationship in this family is. Again, loving concern, communication, and adjustments are necessary on the part of both parents.

What about a man who makes a woman feel ashamed of her body?

I wonder if the man involved in this question realizes that his behavior might be tolling the death knell for his own good sexual experience. Women generally don't have as positive feelings about their bodies as men do about theirs anyway, so anything that further adds to their feelings of inadequacy has the effect of making them want to hide their bodies or make them unavailable.

Generally, someone runs another down because he doesn't feel good about some part of himself. It works something like this: If I feel inadequate and inferior, I need to find someone who I can see as even less acceptable, so I try hard to find flaws in other people.

Since you can't change him simply by willing it—or as you have probably found out, by complaining and fussing—why not try something else? Try this experiment. Every time he "runs you down," retaliate by "running him up." When he says something uncomplimentary about you, compliment him on something that may be completely unrelated. Tune

BEYOND THE "I DO'S"

out his negative, and tune in your positive. Now, I am not suggesting that this is the easiest thing in the world to do; it may well be the hardest for you! But think of it as a scientific experiment. What interesting things could happen! At the very least it could make you feel like you were more in control of the situation, for you will probably become so involved that what he says won't be as defeating.

I don't know if I am talking here to you as a firm size ten or a relaxed size sixteen! But if body improvement would make you feel better about yourself, it might be worth the effort—to you. Do it for yourself.

Another thing might be involved here. Some other parts of your relationship may be the real problem for him. This may just be the "scapegoat" for some conscious or unconscious situations that are bothering him. It would be good to talk this over, which may need a third person in the form of a counselor, a pastor trained in this type of interaction, or a marriage enrichment weekend that concentrates on communication.

Are all women capable of orgasm during intercourse, or must some be further stimulated?

A number of women need stimulation beyond that provided through intercourse. Sometimes this is because the time devoted to love play is minimal and insufficient. But even under ideal circumstances, some women arouse more slowly and need more stimulation. A caution here needs to be mentioned. Clitoral stimulation must be gentle, always with lubricant, and not too directly. Manual caressing around this little piece of body tissue for most women is more stimulating than direct touching.

It's delightful to know that this small piece of tissue in a woman's genital anatomy has for its only purpose to receive and transmit pleasure. Imagine that! All the other parts of men's and women's bodies that have to do with sexuality have more than one function. Not the clitoris! That is a good thing to remember when we think of God's creation as all-purposeful. This means that enjoying sexuality to its fullest was intended to be enjoyed by women just as much as it is by men.

What About Having Children?
Do you believe that sex is for procreation only?

No, I don't. Procreation is only one of the gifts of sexuality—an important one, to be sure. But pleasure is also one of its gifts. In the entire book of the Song of Solomon—that great love poem we have already mentioned—not one word is mentioned about the procreative aspects of sexuality. Pleasure is its only theme. Again in Proverbs 5:18, 19 (NIV) we note this dual quality of sex:

> May your fountain be blessed,
> And may you rejoice in the wife of your youth.
> A loving doe, a graceful deer—
> May her breasts satisfy you always,
> And may you ever be captivated by her love.

Recall too that long after a woman is no longer capable of bearing children, her ability to enjoy sexual experiences is present. Often women past child-bearing age find their desire enhanced. But we will be discussing that part of the life cycle in Chapter 6.

How many years after marriage do you think you should have children?

I am not prepared to give an inflexible number here. I think the circumstances of the couple are more important than a set number of years. However, every child has the right to be born into a home where it is dearly wanted. In addition, parents should be able to provide for it materially and emotionally. For some couples, this combination of circumstances may be a long time coming. Then it's best that they wait. Children should not be brought into the world simply to gratify a desire to be fruitful. Children need to be loved, cherished, and made to feel very special.

What about not having children? Personally I don't want any.

It is good that you realize this before you have children. Far too many parents don't make that discovery until the children are here! A number of young couples have carefully and thoughtfully made the decision not to have children on the basis of their evaluation of themselves as parent material. Others are involved in such absorbing careers that having children would simply mean that others would be rearing them in baby-sitting capacities. Not to have children is a decision that should also be carefully discussed before marriage, so that neither partner is terribly disappointed when they discover what their spouse had in mind even before marriage.

When a couple does make a final decision, it should be made very carefully, since time can run out on the ability to change one's mind. But if the decision is carefully thought through and is not made impetuously or fearfully or selfishly, don't feel you have to explain it to anyone outside your home.

We cannot have children, though we wish we could. For years we have been pressed by church members on this issue. Some ask personal questions, and usually just on Sabbath when they see us. Often I am crying as we leave church. Why don't they leave us alone? (Condensed from a much longer appeal.)

If they could know your feelings, I am sure that they *would* leave you alone. Rarely do people deliberately set out to hurt their fellow church members. Some do it carelessly and thoughtlessly though, little realizing its effect. I include this question in the hope that your experience can help others to see that questions of this nature have no place in our interaction. Fellowshiping together in church should have for its goal the enhancing of our feelings of understanding and regard for one another.

I have yet to hear from one couple who felt that being pressured and questioned on this issue made them decide to have children. That is a poor demonstration of effective techniques to bring about change! Usually the response is negative, though perhaps not as traumatic as the question above suggests.

What does the church say about birth control?

I don't believe that the Seventh-day Adventist Church has made a definitive statement that binds members to any particular course of action. Some of these sensitive areas do not require dogmatic pronouncements. They need careful evaluation by each person making the decision. God Himself introduced some "built-in" birth control. Out of the (usually) twenty-seven to twenty-eight-day menstrual cycle a woman passes through each month, she is capable of being fertilized only during a few hours of that time.

I believe that birth control, when carefully planned with a physician who is aware of the medical situation of the couple, can be a real boon. I further feel that both husbands and wives should be actively involved in that planning and equally responsible for its implementation, whatever that will involve.

Birth control would seem practical, but very unnatural, affecting the attitudes toward sexual relationship.

I am not sure I have found that effective and jointly planned contraception has a negative effect on the sexual relationship of a wife and husband. On the contrary, usually they are both relieved to have the freedom to enjoy their love play without constantly being concerned about a pregnancy resulting.

As for being unnatural, would you consider it unnatural that God directed that fertility in a woman be restricted to a limited time period? Would it be more natural, in your thinking, if she could get pregnant any day of any month?

Actually, the only negative effects I have seen on a marital relationship in this area occur when one wishes a child and the other does not, with resulting anger if contraception is continued. But this is not a contraception problem. It is one that involves difficulties around conflict resolution, negotiation, and communication. This is why I so strongly urge premarital counseling. So much misunderstanding and trouble might be avoided. Alas, far too often this does not take place.

BEYOND THE "I DO'S"

Problems of Infidelity

For many years and without reason my mate has accused me of adultery. I cannot respond to his sexual desires anymore because of his jealousy.

Jealousy can destroy not only the sexual aspect of a marriage, but the total relationship. Perhaps that is why Paul is careful to propose several qualities of love that are completely incompatible with jealousy. Love always protects, always trusts, and always hopes.

While your husband's accusation is bringing you unhappiness, you can be sure he also feels miserable. When he sees you as nonresponsive, this in turn makes him more sure that he is right and that you are experiencing sexual fulfillment with someone else. Perhaps he needs more reassurance that you love him. Perhaps earlier his feelings about himself may have been sufficient to sustain his self-concept. Maybe this has been attacked by work problems, financial concerns, worries over the children, etc. The worse he feels about himself, the more he may be trying to convince himself that you are not a good person.

Granted, it's very difficult to be loving and giving when he is accusing you. If it's impossible to discuss this together on a helpful level, I would suggest counseling for you. Even if he refuses, you could be helped to learn how to cope and how best to respond so that you don't keep slipping into discouragement and withdrawal. There is more to marriage than just "sticking it out." Marriage was meant to be a source of companionship and pleasure. You may have to be the first one to take steps toward this goal.

How can you forgive a husband who has been unfaithful? I just can't forget.

Forgiveness is not something you can manufacture at will. It is something that God gives to those who seek it. Somehow the sin of infidelity seems the most difficult to grant forgiveness for. It seems to be at the top of a hierarchy of things that are bad. Maybe at a past time your husband has asked you to forgive him for a temper outburst or some other indiscretion, and you found it possible to do that. Here, in this situation, you seem to be stuck.

Forgiveness is a matter of the will and not of the feelings. Perhaps you have already found that there are times when this resistance is worse than others. Try to figure out what has happened. Are these unforgiving times when you yourself have experienced insecurity the result of something else in another area troubling you? What is going on when you feel this way? You and your husband need to discuss this, and talk over what he can do to build your sense of trust and confidence. Most men in your husband's situation are eager to help their wives put aside their painful feelings.

Remember that forgiveness doesn't mean feeling good; there will still be occasional twinges of pain. But these will diminish with time, for we are made to heal, not only physically but emotionally. Our part in helping a physical wound to heal is to allow it to rest. Try to think of that treatment for your emotional wound.

My husband and I are separated, and he is living with another woman. He calls often to say that if I will just promise to guarantee meeting his sexual needs, he might reconsider reconciliation.

To suggest that marriages can be healed, or even kept together, just by meeting sexual needs is a very simplistic idea. Good sexual interaction will enhance a marriage, but it rarely is the cause of its breakup. Many, many couples who do not have Class A sex stay together happily, for they have many good things going for them. Many couples who do have Class A sex separate. Sex alone is not enough to hold marriages together if they are deeply troubled in other areas.

I think your husband needs to do some thinking about his part in the separation and realize that his bargaining attitude is a poor offering in exchange for your cooperation. You both need to realize that his affair is the result of problems in your relationship. Both of you should have a clearer picture of what these are before you ever undertake reuniting your lives.

Hearing from him seems to be painful to you by resurrecting your hopes only to dash them again. I would suggest that for the present you ask him not to call until he has something more helpful to discuss. Instead of allowing him to disturb you by going through his "offer" again, simply say something like this: "I don't believe we have anything to discuss unless we can work with a third person to find out why all this happened in the first place." A counselor could help you sort out the issues involved, and this could be a very good place for you to start, even by yourself. Meanwhile, firmly resist being drawn into these painful discussions with him unless he can meet your request.

Why does an apparently totally surrendered Christian husband in an otherwise ideal relationship seem to constantly look for and savor the sight of the opposite sex in "scanty" attire?

Many women have a hard time understanding this phenomenon! Since women generally are not avidly attracted to men based on their physiques—in whatever state of undress—it is hard for them to see why men eagerly seek to view scantily attired women. But then, men find it hard to understand why women think feelings and emotions are so desirable, and can't comprehend why women put so much emphasis on this part of a relationship.

I am going to forego the explanation about how some men do this to needle, heckle, humiliate, and upset their wives. This doesn't fit in with your description of your Christian husband, though it is true of some situations.

Let's face it, our culture teaches men that they are supposed to be agog and eager! When they are not, they are often seen by other men as somehow missing a cylinder. When "appreciation" turns into lust, then we are faced with another problem. Perhaps if more husbands realized how their wives are sometimes diminished and concerned when their husbands show so much response to this type of "looking," they could soft-pedal their eagerness and spend more time appreciating their wives' physical qualities. Wives don't want their husbands to ignore female beauty altogether. They just want them to use restraint in their remarks over the beauty of other women's bodies!

Is genuine love between a husband and wife a guarantee that they will not be sexually attracted to other people?

I think it would be safe to say that. But how often do we have examples of "genuine love" in this mixed-up, tottering world? Only God's love is genuine and perfect. It would be safer to say that both wives and husbands should ever be watchful of their level of commitment to be sexually faithful. This would include thoughtfully and prayerfully erecting standards for their own thinking and behavior. But most of all, it would urge wives and husbands to consistently work to improve their offerings of love to one another. That shouldn't be a tough assignment, because we are so well rewarded by a spouse who is doing exactly the same thing for us.

Should a married man have a female friend as his sounding board?

I guess that would depend on what he is trying to sound out! Perhaps in the business world, working on problems of job performance, this could be helpful. On a church committee, the exchange of ideas over church concerns could be useful and stimulating. However, if you mean on a personal, emotional issue, I would advise caution. If all the energy that husbands and wives spent talking with others about their marital problems could be focused in on their *own* with *their* spouses, what a blessing that would be!

While I am writing this, I am remembering both husbands and wives who have told me that their spouses had long since stopped really listening to them. Instead they argued, contradicted, cajoled, or acted bored. Many affairs start from the need to have someone who will truly listen. From this the relationship drifts into physical activity.

Husbands and wives often need to stop and ask themselves, "When is the last time I listened to my spouse completely, with every bit of my attention?" This is manifested by good eye contact, expectant posture, and occasional "verbal enhancers" like: "Hm," "Oh, I see," "Hey, that's interesting," or "I'd like to hear more about that." You come back for more when someone is that interested in what you are saying. If the spouse is not, someone out there will be!

Being best friends and serving as "sounding boards" are two of the neat things about marriage. We need to cultivate those "tasks" with all our energies.

If a married person is *entirely* selfish—couldn't this be a form of adultery—the person being married to self rather than to the other person?

What an interesting thought, one which a committee considering a restudy of the *Church Manual* might do well to ponder. Let's think this through. A totally selfish person would have regard for no one but him or herself. He or she would want to benefit no interest but her or his own. The feelings of the other would not ever be considered. Lack of regard might even be manifested in verbal, or even physical abuse. Such a person could scarcely be considered faithful to the marriage vows that he or she proclaimed "in the presence . . ."

I believe we need an extended study of marital "unfaithfulness." And maybe we shouldn't wait for a committee to do it. We could each explore that idea for ourselves and for the good of our own marriages, not to figure out a way to escape the marriage but to improve it.

Chapter 5

The Anniversaries Go By

Questions in this chapter have separated themselves from the last one, which were asked more often by young married adults. Those asking the questions in this chapter identified themselves by the number of years they had been married (which we shall omit) or by other information which will not be supplied. You will notice that many of them speak to what seems to be a need for revitalization of the marriage in the area of sexuality. Others indicate that perhaps things had never been ideal.

Nothing is surer than this: couples need to be ever aware that marriages do not stay great all by themselves without attention from both wives and husbands. The press of the dailiness of living, with all the stresses and problems that absolutely no one is immune to, can dull the hopes and dreams that the starry-eyed bride and groom left the altar with. We have to keep "stoking the fires"—which is exactly what Ellen White, one of my favorite authors, said. Here is that charming statement, "Love can no more exist without revealing itself in outward acts than fire can be kept alive without fuel." She was writing, by the way, in a letter to a gentleman whom she characterizes as not manifesting tenderness and affection to his wife. She also suggested to him that his lack of these behaviors had made both of their lives "wretched."

Let's do away with wretched, cold, inconsiderate marriages! Let's revive the "tired blood" of such relationships. Studies have shown that when the interpersonal relationship is not good, sexuality will be affected. Only ashes of what could be a warm, caring, experience are left when there is no fuel for the fire. Too many couples have discovered this to be true, as the questions below will show.

102

Revitalization

> **My husband does not act as warm, tender, and loving anymore. He does not respond to my tender approaches. He is cold. When I ask him why, he says married couples should not act like those people who are still dating.**

You know, he's right! Married couples should *not* act like couples who date. They should be so much more loving, considerate, and caring that it would be easy to identify them in any crowd! You use the word *anymore*, so I am assuming that once he was more demonstrative. I wonder if some event in your lives may have been a beginning point for this new behavior. Was there a job change or disappointment? Financial problems? An illness that necessitated him taking medications which may have affected his energy level, even his sex drive? Perhaps he doesn't feel good about himself generally.

If it's been a more gradual change, I wonder if you both have allowed the stresses and strains of living to cause you to neglect having fun together, accompanied by playful teasing and laughter. Without these, sometimes people begin to feel "old" and act as they think old people should.

Since you can't mandate a change in him, *you* may have to initiate some of these rituals again. Is that fair? Should one person have to make all the effort? No, it's not fair. But who said life was fair? Besides, it's more important to *be* on the right track than to *keep* on track. In your own mind, make a game of seeing how long it will take for the change to make a difference in him—all, of course, without divulging your plan or acting virtuous about your mature behavior! You will feel better about yourself and recognize how this affects others around you.

> **Why are men so unromantic? Why won't they do the little things to keep their wives happy?**

Let me go to bat for men here, because some men *are* romantic, even after twenty, thirty-five, and forty-seven years of marriage! But what you want to know is why *your* husband isn't romantic. I wish I knew. But let me venture some ideas.

Perhaps he came from a home where romance was completely unimportant. Loving behaviors may have been considered childish, even ridiculous. If a man has never seen a living example of loving attentions, if he has never heard verbal expressions demonstrating caring, he really doesn't have much to serve as a model. Oh, but you say, "I've told him over and over and over what I mean!" You know, it's just possible that by now you have begun to sound nagging, impatient, and critical. It may have assumed the proportions of a power play and to yield would be a sign of weakness, of giving in.

In all honesty, we should look at what part you could possibly play in this situation. Do you keep yourself attractive, fragrant, and lovable, even when you are home alone? Do you compliment him frequently? Do you subtly suggest things you would like him to do: "You know, I was thinking of how nice it would be if I could hear you call me when you first get home, and I could leave what I am doing and come and give you a big welcoming hug!" Then change the subject and don't let it hang on the air as if he had to respond.

You're right, a wife needs "little things" to give her a feeling of specialness, of being appreciated and cherished. If men really understood this and the dividends it would pay, they would promptly turn romantic! Sometimes men actually do not know *how* to be romantic and need examples and feedback from their wives. Why not make a list of all the little things you consider romantic. Show him the list, and ask him, if he were to make a list of ways you could be romantic, would some of these same things be on it? Make it a lighthearted experience, timed to follow some especially satisfying time together.

What about a man who says that as long as he gets sex (with his wife) as often as he wants, everything else will be OK?

OK for whom? Since this question seems to have been turned in by his wife, I am pretty sure that it's not OK with her! Besides, I am concerned about what it seems to be saying. Is sex supposed to be some kind of a fix-all remedy, a preventive measure, a prescription? Should a wife be pleased to be a sexual partner just to keep things on an even

THE ANNIVERSARIES GO BY

keel? Or should sex be a mutual response to a good interpersonal relationship based on mutual love?

This, and earlier questions, do point out to us the differences with which men and women sometimes look at sexuality. A woman is much more likely to wish intercourse to be an outgrowth of a warm, loving relationship. In fact, studies have shown that when a woman feels good about the way her husband meets her needs for loving, cherishing, and respect, several things follow. She is more likely to be orgasmic, to want sex more often, and to agree on the course of lovemaking. She is also more likely to see her husband as a good lover—not because of his techniques, but because of his attitudes. Men might want to study that list! When they realize what wonderful results can come from tenderness, thoughtfulness, and time together—the Big Three T's—they can realize how much better sexuality can be for them too.

My wife acts like she is doing me a favor to have sex with me.

Here is the other side of the coin! Women are not alone in wishing their partners were more responsive. Let's conjecture what might be going on here. As she was growing up, perhaps her home messages told her that sexually, men were always out to get what they could. Women had to keep them in line by dampening their passions. This is pretty much what women in our culture were being told several generations back, and would you believe it, some still hear this message?

Your wife may have had some unpleasant childhood experiences. It is also possible that early in marriage she was disappointed in lovemaking and found it too eager, too fast, and too quiet. This happened not because you were deliberately inconsiderate, but because no one had given you helpful information about sexuality. Your wife may not be quite sure that God intended her to be thrilled and responsive in sexuality. Many wives are not sure that ecstasy is heaven-approved.

I am going to suggest that you initiate a low-key, non-threatening conversation with her, asking her if there is anything on your part that might make her feel less than positive about sex. Don't be defensive or upset at her reply. Just listen, and thank her for telling you. Allow her to say what is on her heart without interruption.

If her feelings predated your relationship, let her get out all the negative feelings that you are not responsible for. Then try to court her all over again. It is possible that the two of you might need some professional help to unravel this knot. But it will be worth it when you are both looking forward to and enjoying the pleasure of one another.

How can you get intimacy and lightheartedness back in a relationship once it is gone?

What a hopeful question! Here is someone who realizes that through the years something has happened. She remembers when they used to laugh and tease and have fun together. Perhaps that was when they were courting or first married. Then what so often happens, happened to them. With the arrival of children and the responsibilities of mortgages and car payments, life began to seem very serious, and the joy disappeared. No one should try to convince you that life is *not* earnest and real. It is! But lots of room remains for happy times too.

Even God's good friend David, who went through a list of tribulations that few of us will ever meet—some of his own making, of course—was so overcome with delight and exuberance that sometimes he danced with joy! Many times in his songs, he instructs us—even insists—that we rejoice and be glad—be exceedingly glad!

Now, what to do when it seems to have disappeared. You have taken the first step in recognizing the problem and expressing a desire to make it different. It will be easier if you are also speaking for your spouse. But it is not impossible even if you are the only one who feels the need for change.

Write a list of all the things that used to be lighthearted and fun for the two of you. Some of these may have changed with new circumstances, but jot them down anyway. Then continue the list with things that you think would add to your joint pleasures now. Maybe your list will include things like reading a humorous book out loud together, hiking, baking cookies together, visiting friends, playing games, going window shopping at the mall, cutting out cartoons and jokes to share with one another, planning a vacation together with the help of library resources, visiting museums, art galleries, zoos, memorials in your state, playing catch on the lawn, taking a trip to a swimming pool, spending an evening a week at a health club, or it may be snatching a five-minute hugging session on the couch—just like you used to do when you thought no one was looking before you were married. You could go on and on.

Note that there is no mention of watching television. I have my own conviction that the television sets in our homes have taken away from the interaction between family members. The only way television could help out in this venture is if you plan in advance what you are going to look at, sit down together with a cool lemonade, and then turn it off afterward and discuss what you saw. Now just a minute! How come talking about discussing it seems to be such a drag now? Remember all the times you used to love to discuss things with your special date? (At least, that is what you told your parents you did!) When talking about experiences now seems dull, it may be because we have allowed our minds to stagnate. If we are still curious and interested, and have viewpoints that keep expanding, we will love to listen to one another. We won't always agree, but we can have the fun of championing our causes!

Back to the list. If this is a solo venture, put it up on the refrigerator or someplace easily visible, with an invitation to "look over this list when you have time and see what you think of it." If you get no response for a few days, suggest that you are going to choose one for both of you, or yourself alone, if necessary. Then do it. Have such a good time, and come home with a new sparkle. Wait to see how long it will take before you get some enthusiasm going both ways. It won't happen the day after tomorrow. But if you are persistent and bring a note of adventure and humor into it, it will work.

Problem Areas of the Physical Kind

Sometimes my husband loses his erection. What would cause this? Does it mean I'm not sexually appealing enough? Or is it just that he is overtired?

First it should be stated that all men, at one time or another, lose an erection. The reason may be as dramatic as someone shouting, "Fire!" or as routine as a small child crying over a bad dream. Erections are an involuntary response to sexual stimulation and cannot be willed to come or go. It is only human for you to feel that you lack the sexual appeal to bring about your husband's erection. But don't take that responsibility, unless of course you have deliberately insulted, angered, or belittled him. But I do not believe that to be the situation here.

You have cited one of the reasons that erections are lost, and a very important one. Fatigue is a real bedroom enemy! So is boredom, which would be no more your responsibility than his. But if you have an unvarying routine for your love play month after month, year after year, it can become unexciting enough to lose an erection over!

Another reason could be a physical condition, such as might result from taking a medication known to depress sexual response. (Warning! Do not leave off any medications until a doctor is consulted. If a medication could be responsible, your physician can probably prescribe an alternative one. If your doctor does not seem particularly interested or concerned about medicine that may be causing a sexual slow-down, you may want to consult a more cooperative one. Most doctors are willing to work with you on this.)

Men sometimes do not realize that as they grow older, certain physical changes can occur. (See the next chapter for a more detailed discussion of this.) It may take a little longer for an adequate erection to take place, and more stimulation may be necessary. In other words, the whole process of having a sexual love-in may take longer. Isn't that good news? Now you have a real reason to make love longer and take more time in pleasing one another.

But when a man first begins to realize that he is not ready quite as quickly, he begins to worry about it. The worry causes him to take up "self-spectatoring." Rather than enjoying and experiencing his sexual responses, he starts to wonder if it is going to happen and if his erection is going to be as good as it used to be. Then this worry and concern can

THE ANNIVERSARIES GO BY

affect the quality of the erection. It won't be his physical ability that is causing the problem.

Perhaps he also needs some verbal expression from you telling him how much his lovemaking means to you. He will benefit by knowing that he has not failed as a lover. Perhaps he also would appreciate more active initiation on your part to follow through and confirm this.

This is a good place to pause and say something about the whole lovemaking sequence. Too often couples concentrate on the intercourse part of lovemaking, as though it were the most important and vital part of being together. This might be true when children are wanted, but in this age group, that is probably not the case! Some couples for years have concentrated on intercourse and orgasms and relegated all the other wonderful touching, caressing, hugging, kissing, stroking, rubbing, cuddling parts of lovemaking to a lesser role. Later, when lovemaking could be slowed down and enjoyed, they aren't accustomed to that.

Many husbands do not realize that for most wives, these touching pleasures are so desirable that they would rather give up intercourse than these, if they had to make that choice. Often husbands who have never given much importance to these loving touches find it is really great for them, too, when they get into the spirit of it.

What if a man is impotent but very eager to have sex? What is the best way to satisfy the wife?

A man with continuing erectile problems does not have erections firm enough to make intercourse possible. This can be a great trauma for a man to experience. Our culture has made men feel that to be worthwhile, they must be virile. Be they ever so kind, loving, rich, or famous, if they are not also sexually capable, they are taught to feel like failures. Women do not experience anything quite so devastating. They have the physical capacity to be a receiving partner, even though it may not be enjoyable. A woman is not nearly as likely to measure her value by this ability. This means a man loses both ways. If his wife doesn't have orgasms, it's his fault; if he doesn't have erections, it's also his fault. That's a pretty heavy load to carry.

A man experiencing erection failure should be physically examined to make certain that there are no medical problems. In the past, it was believed that erection problems usually had a psychological background. Now we recognize that there can also be physical reasons, and these should be checked out before further action is taken. Today doctors say that it would be a good idea for men to have yearly genital examinations, too, to rule out conditions that could become serious if unchecked. Most doctors will also take a sexual history to find if there are any differences in sexual capacities, and this can open the way for a discussion of the erectile problems.

If it is determined that these problems are not medically treatable, then the couple has several choices. They can consult a qualified person who specializes in sexual therapy to discover if there are some hidden roadblocks in the relationship or in individual attitudes and thinking. This can be very helpful. They can also consult a urologist, who will inform them about the prostheses now available which can make an erection mechanically possible. There are several newer appliances that make this a much more attractive option than it used to be.

An alternative is to decide that they have so many good things going for them in their marriage that they are going to make the most of the plateau part of their lovemaking. They can emphasize the stimulation they can give one another through—well, by now you can repeat them, so I will just say touching, etc.! The husband's caressing of his wife's genitals can be effective in releasing her sexual tensions. This is not masturbation, or what is sometimes called mutual masturbation. Both are incorrect terms for this type of lovemaking. Masturbation is a solo pursuit of self-gratification. This is mutual stimulation, which has for its goal bringing pleasure that would otherwise not be possible when intercourse is not an alternative. This comes from the husband's concern for his wife's needs and brings them into a closeness they could not otherwise enjoy.

My husband has the problem of not ejaculating very soon, and sometimes he won't stop trying until it is very painful for me. He says just a little longer.

This condition is known as retarded ejaculation and is on the opposite end of the continuum from premature ejaculation. Once he is aroused, it sometimes takes long periods of thrusting for a man to finally ejaculate, if he ever does. This can be, as you describe, very painful for the wife. It then causes her to want to withdraw and have nothing more to do with intercourse. Of course, this means that playful and meaningful behaviors, usually such a pleasure for husbands and wives, are curtailed so that they won't lead into intercourse. The more the wife resists, the more driven the husband becomes, and you can see what a vicious circle this can be.

This state of things is not anymore pleasant for a sensitive husband than it is for his wife. He would much rather be a lover who not only gets what he wants, but considers her. It may not seem that way when you are in the middle of sexual interaction, but I am sure that it is true. No doubt he has thought: have that ejaculation, or you have failed as a man.

Some "behind the scenes" problems occasionally promote retarded ejaculation. It would be good for you to get counsel from a qualified person about this. You may both be involved in whatever is causing this, and I am sure you are eager to find out what your part could be. Please persist until you find someone who can help turn things around for you, so that you can both be willing and eager lovers again.

Is there injury to a man who is not allowed to ejaculate after he has been aroused?

The good news is, No. Having said that, let me add that if a man should have repeated episodes of arousal almost to orgasm without ejaculation, there could be a discomfort and heaviness in the scrotal region. Some men are relieved through involuntary nocturnal emissions. Some are not. Others have been programmed to believe that depriving themselves of ejaculations every time will cause immediate discomfort. For them, then, it happens! (Let us add here that any continuing feelings of discomfort in the scrotal area should certainly be medically investigated.)

Older men will particularly feel less urgency and engorgement than younger men. Isn't that good news for those adding years? Some men report that they can feel a great deal of satisfaction from love play that does not go into ejaculations. For them orgasms are not necessary every time that they make love.

Should a Christian wife try to arouse her husband's sex drive?

I think I am hearing suggestions of an attitude that is not comfortable with Christians getting too sexy! Or maybe it questions whether wives should be involved in sexual drives—that it might be all right for Christian husbands to arouse their wives, but not for Christian wives to arouse their husbands.

First, let's remember that the whole area of sex drives, sex needs, and sexual satisfaction was not thought up by Christians at all, but by God. It was His idea from beginning to end. It was His plan that both husbands and wives could be aroused by certain stimuli, certain signals from their spouses, and both could be stimulated to the point of climax. This implanted passion is so strong that even after the original Edenic fall, after which so many factors fought against sex being the wonderful experience God intended it to be, God predicted that wives would still desire their husbands (see Genesis 3:16).

We have already referred to Song of Solomon in previous chapters, but let's recall here that in that whole recitation of love between the beloved and the lover, she (the beloved) spoke of her love more enticingly. She was given a larger part in the recorded dialogue than her lover.

My concept of sexuality as God intended it to be includes an active involvement by *both* husband and wife. Each should seek to demonstrate a loving commitment to the other as participating equals. Because of the way God created us, we are each aroused by the other's sexuality even on an unconscious level. Let us also enjoy this capability on a conscious level.

THE ANNIVERSARIES GO BY

After ___ years of marriage, the excitement as first experienced is struggling to survive. The present experience is successful, but not as much fun as it used to be.

It's only natural that the experience of sexuality is going to change through the years. Everything else does; life is always in process. Some older lovers report that now that they have made love to one another for a number of years, they have learned so much about one another's responses, feel so much more open, and communicate so much better, that sex has never been better. They declare they wouldn't trade what they have now for a return to earlier days. A question like this one makes us realize that there are other effects of years slipping by. For some, the eager, passionate days look much better by comparison.

Isn't it possible to have some of each—excitement *and* security? Passion *and* companionship? Perhaps the satisfied lovers have never allowed their sexuality to become ho-hum. They still surprise one another with notes under the pillow, perfume sprayed on pillowslips, or a new negligee. Playfully hiding the pajamas, a scented candle, romantic music, reading love poetry together, showering together, bubble-bathing one another tenderly—these are only some of the many ways to put the excitement back.

It won't happen by itself. Husbands and wives have a part in making love time special. You'd feel silly introducing some of these ideas after all these years? Do it anyway. It could bring back the excitement you miss.

We are so bombarded by the world's brand of sex that I feel like I am competing with the world when we have sex.

I think I know what you mean. We are confronted with so much that is unrealistic, ugly, and violent that it is sometimes difficult to think of this as having anything to do with God's plan. The whole world has departed from His blueprint. But that is true of many other aspects of our lives as well—marriage, parenting, ecological stewardship—

we see deviations in all of these, too.

We constantly try to remind ourselves of God's plan for us in any area by reading His guidebook, talking with Him, and fellowshiping with others who believe as we do. This helps us to stay sensitive to the blueprint. Why not get involved in His guidelines for our sexual outlook?

Secure either the New King James Version or the New International Version of the Bible. Then some evening when you have *at least* thirty to forty minutes of time and have had a relaxing shower or bath, crawl into bed together, putting your pillows up against the headboard so you can sit up, leaning on them. Place a goblet of sparkling cider or grape juice on each of your bedstands. Then turn to the book Song of Solomon. You will note that it is divided into words that are spoken by the beloved and the lover. Read the lines that fit your sex—the wife is the beloved, the husband is the lover. You will note that some lines are not dialogue, but are descriptions. Read these in unison together. Sip your juice leisurely as you read along until you have gone through the entire book, or poem.

I feel this will help you put into perspective what God hopes sexuality will mean to a husband and wife. The world will continue to degrade this gift, as it has many of God's other gifts. But you will be able to keep your mind on the ideal—"Whatsoever is beautiful . . ."

What suggestions do you have for that time period in married life when husbands go into midlife crisis, and they're telling their wives they don't love them anymore? The marriage, they say, was a mistake. They are tired of the children and the pressures of staying in the marriage relationship when someone younger is looking better to them.

Though this situation refers to husbands, sometimes it is a woman who says she is done with the responsibility of marriage and mothering and wants out. Whatever the circumstances, it represents a lot of pain for both spouses. No marital partner can easily and lightly leave the family without confusion, disorganization, and conflict.

Sometimes the marriage was undertaken at a young age. Now one spouse is feeling gypped for not having had a chance to "get around" in the world—both socially and professionally—before getting involved in responsibility. Persons who had big dreams and lofty goals feel that they are passing a time when it will be possible to see any of these fulfilled unless they leave their marriage encumbrances and try it on their own. Lack of tender care for the marriage relationship by one or both partners may have robbed it of so much meaning that someone wants out.

Go slowly! Do not make abrupt decisions on what you want to do, e.g., leave, throw the bum out, call a lawyer, etc. These decisions might be based more on anger and revenge than clear, careful thinking. Blaming, yelling, preaching, scolding, shaming—none of these will be helpful, so save your energy and leave these easy responses alone. Rather, I suggest trying to understand, giving feelings of continued support and hope (regardless of what happens), and waiting—and sometimes waiting again.

That's expecting too much of anyone, you say. It does seem so, doesn't it? But there is no easy fix for a problem like this. You will come out of this a different person, and you will be the one to choose how it will be for you. You can be angry, beaten-down, hopeless, and embittered. Or you can pull together your resources. These can include first of all your heavenly Father, then your earthly family, your church, and your friends. (Your husband will not have the same quality of resources as you do; you are the fortunate one.) You may find it even more helpful to discuss this in therapy with an objective person. Use any resource you can.

Whether the marriage reknits or not, I hope you will come out a more mature person. You may also find that as time elapses, the wayward spouse will respond to the strong pull of the family unit. If so, don't expect it to be automatically wonderful. Some things will still need to be worked through, perhaps in counseling. As difficult as it will be, refrain from going back with blame, censure, and self-pity. Be glad for the miracle of reunion. With God's help, make it the best new start that you can.

Chapter 6

No Retirement Age For Sexuality

In many younger people's minds, sexual experiences are no longer the repertoire of their aging parents and certainly not their grandparents! Because this attitude is so prevalent, evidenced by remarks, anecdotes, and jokes (which I believe to be in very poor taste), sometimes older folk tend to be embarrassed about their needs and desires. Frequently they stifle what they are feeling to fit into the stereotype of a properly neutered senior citizen. But sexuality is not metered by a calendar. Actually, I can give many reasons why the sexuality of older persons can be more rewarding and significant than at any other time in their lives.

For one thing, worry about pregnancy, which can hamper good sex in younger persons, is no longer a concern. With the children departed to start their own homes, privacy is easier. Over the years, seniors have had the opportunity—and we hope they use it—to develop better communication and understanding. Therefore a fuller expression of needs and desires is present. Some of the earlier inhibitions are now released, so they can feel freer in their sexual expression.

In spite of these positive forces, unfortunately many times in later years we find a decline or even an abandoning of sexual activity. This not only includes intercourse, but the entire gamut of sexual experience. Men are more likely to have the philosophy that if you can't do it like you used to, don't even start what you can't finish. Strangely, they are using this as a reason to be asexual even when their wives are longing for the nonintercourse activities of sexuality—the hugging, kissing, caressing, and snuggling.

Often this happens because neither one understands the sexual changes that occur in aging for what they are—not a death blow, simply a slowing down. And they come at a time

NO RETIREMENT AGE FOR SEXUALITY

in life when they at last have more time. What could be more appropriate?

Many other physical abilities are experiencing changes. Why not sexuality? Sight, hearing, the ability to climb two flights of stairs on the run—all of these are now different than earlier; why should sexuality be an exception?

But let's look at this group of questions from retirees (a word I like so much better than senior citizens, now that I am one!).

Loss of Sexual Desire
What shall I do? I have lost interest in sex.

First, I commend you for wanting to do something about it, not just accepting your lack of interest as inevitable. If you read previous chapters in this book, you have noted that we have already discussed some reasons why people are no longer interested in this part of their relationship. But in this section, let's talk about one factor that I think is very important for people in your age group. If we do not clearly understand what sexual changes are perfectly natural for those growing older, when we recognize the signals we think we are over-the-hill! Finished! People feel incapable, undesirable, and "worn-out," and they settle for spending the rest of their lives without sexual contact.

Most studies, by the way, indicate that sexual desire persists for both women and men well into the seventies and eighties, and a good number of persons in the nineties still have an active sexual interest.

But now, let's have a look at some of the changes that will occur, first for women. A woman may notice that it takes somewhat longer for her to reach full sexual desire. In other words, a longer time of stimulation will be required, which is something she has usually wanted anyway! Less lubrication may be available, but this is easily supplied by many fine preparations on the market (not petroleum jelly or cold cream—these are not water soluble and could cause problems). The orgasmic phase may be somewhat shortened, but this will not take away from the feeling of gratification and satisfaction. Occasionally a woman may experience discomfort with intercourse due to the thinning of the vaginal wall, but her doctor can prescribe a cream preparation that will alleviate this problem. Women who have engaged in regular sexual activity through the years show fewer of the above symptoms.

Sometimes when a man recognizes these changes in his wife, he feels that somehow he is responsible for them because he is not as exciting a lover as he used to be. This concern could bring about a slowing-down in his own functioning and add to the problem. Concern for what a woman perceives as her diminishing sexual ability can provoke anxiety for her, but it does not interfere with her ability to be a physical partner. This is not true of her husband. When he becomes preoccupied and worried about the physical quality of his sexual response, he can actually worry an otherwise able body into erectile impotence. When that happens, some men give up *any* expression of sexuality whatsoever—all hugging and pleasuring and touching and stimulating their wives.

Some changes would not overwhelm a man if he could recognize them as natural events. Generally, the readiness for a quick erection is affected. It will take a longer time and more direct stimulation for the penis to become erect. What formerly happened in seconds may now require several minutes—but who's counting? The penis may be less firm, straight, or large than it was at a younger age, but none of these changes need interfere with a good sexual experience. Men who have formerly had trouble with early ejaculation may find this problem has been helped. Those men who have small amounts of lubricating fluid emitting from their penises prior to ejaculation may find that this diminishes or disappears.

An older man may notice a briefer period of awareness—the moment of "inevitability" just before ejaculation. The intensity of orgasm may undergo some changes, though this may scarcely be noticed. One of the most significant changes is the length of the refractory period, or the time lapse between one ejaculation and the ability to enter again into an intercourse experience.

As you look at these changes, you can easily see that they are not spelling doom to good sex at all. They are asking for a little more time from both husbands and wives in their lovemaking, and that is not all bad! In fact, now that they are retirees, they *have* more time to engage in love play, so it should work out fine.

Again, if a wife is not aware of the possibility of these changes in her husband, she might blame herself for not being as "sexy" as she used to be. She may feel that she somehow lacks the ability to bring about the sexual responses in her husband that she recalls from their earlier lovemaking. If both believe that sex is really not sex without intercourse and orgasm, they will need to do some rethinking. If they have not learned the joys of touching, caressing, cuddling, snuggling, and stroking through the years, they will want to practice these wonderful behaviors. In doing so, they will discover that their life together can be as richly sexual as it ever was. Some consider it even better.

Here is an interesting thing to remember, especially for men. When women were asked in a study: "If from this point on in your life you would have to give up one of two experiences, which one would you want to retain?" Then they were given the choice between having all the love play they want (you remember that this is the term I prefer to foreplay), but having no more orgasms, *or* they could have all the orgasms they wished to have, but without any love play whatsoever. All the women chose the love play! This does not mean that women don't dearly enjoy orgasms, but to take away love play wasn't worth it!

This should help men realize how important it is to spend time in these nonintercourse love activities. All these loving attentions—and I am going to repeat them once more for emphasis: caressing, hugging, stroking, cuddling, nuzzling, kissing, snuggling—all should often be present in couple interaction, aside from, as well as along with, intercourse.

Now back to the original question. We have discussed several reasons why interest in sex might be lost at your age. Check back to see if these sound like something you need to consider. Make sure that you reject feedback from your friends that carries negative messages about sex for older people. Think positively about you and your husband together. Recall the times when you were full of desire, and live again those wonderful experiences. Remember them in detail. Then begin to initiate more loving touching, and encourage your husband to do so too. You two may be delighted to find that an old spark can be rekindled.

Can there be such a thing as too much touching? Even when we don't have sex, my husband is always trying to touch sensitive areas (nipples, clitoris). After all these years I think I deserve a rest.

Maybe what you are saying is not that you don't like any touching, but that you don't like the kind of touching you are getting. I wonder if rubbing your back, cuddling with you, simply lying in one another's arms, would seem like too much touching. I rather think not.

Men sometimes do not realize how very, very sensitive these areas can be. They are not meant to be directly handled or felt independent of other bonding stages of love play. Most women would respond negatively to that.

Your husband may not understand that the clitoris is simply abounding with nerve endings that are extremely sensitive. This tiny little piece of tissue on the upper, outer aspect of the vagina needs very gentle attention. It should not be touched without lubrication or with any degree of roughness, or even firmness. This can not only be uncomfortable, but downright unpleasant.

Sometimes men are overeager and overactive when they are somewhat unsure of themselves as lovers. The sensitive areas you mention usually give more evidence of response than other parts of the body, which seem to make men want to go for them. This gives them assurance that they are effective in getting a sexual response. Unfortunately, all too often the response is opposite to what they want, and literally turns their wives off.

In trying to get your message over to him, remember that he probably does not want to deliberately make you uncomfortable or distressed. He probably just wants to try once more to see if it will provoke some real response from you. Explain to him that your body responds pretty much the same as other women's bodies do, and that this is not a pleasant feeling. Tell him you are sure he does not want to make you feel upset, so you are going to let him know how you would like him to touch you. Sometimes both wives and husbands need to do some repair work on how they present their needs and wishes to their lovers. Also, *do* let him know how good it feels when he does things you like and how that makes you feel so happy that you are married to a good lover. Compliment him in other areas too, so that he can feel good about himself—something each of us needs so much.

My husband says we might as well not sleep together if we can't make love.

Questions like this sadden me. It points out again the prevalent idea that all there is to sexuality for a wife and husband is intercourse, and if you can't have that, nothing else is worth the effort!

Let me give you a little resumé of the benefits of sleeping together in the same bed. First, side by side you slide under the sheets in an acknowledgement of weariness—you deserve this rest, and you deserve the privilege of being able to refresh your tired bodies together. You can now share your last thoughts of the day, going over its especially good parts and the things you could have done without! Of all the people in the world, you would rather have your spouse there than anyone else—and rejoice, you do! You can cuddle and fit into one another's posture, spoon-fashion, or whatever feels best to the two of you. As you turn during the night in a half-asleep awareness, you can reach out a hand or a foot to reassure yourself that you are together, and then drift back to sleep. You can awaken together in the morning, feeling the closeness of your lover, and realizing that you are the only one in the world who has this privilege. That's what sleeping together does for two people.

Now, to use this same space sometimes to consummate that love is certainly wonderful. But when either of you considers that to be the only reason to sleep together, you are cheating your relationship! Maybe your husband will reconsider his bedtime possibilities when he reads this. I hope so!

Do you think you lose your sex desire in the middle fifties? I did.

If you mean, does everyone lose their sexual desires in the middle fifties, the answer is no. Many people are still sexually active in their sixties, seventies, eighties, and even nineties. However, sometimes a function slowdown occurs, as we mentioned in an earlier question, and many times couples do not desire to have sex as often as they did when they were younger.

Let us report, too, that there are couples in their fifties who no longer have intercourse at all. But then this is true of couples both older and younger. For some it is a relief, for they never did find pleasure in their sexual relationship. This can happen for one reason or another, many of which we have already discussed earlier in this book. Others never did have a demanding sex drive, so that over time, intercourse has just dwindled from their repertoire. When both are agreeable to this, it will obviously not be a problem to them.

The problem will be: Does this mean the end of closeness, intimacy, and a sense of exclusive loving? Love play and intercourse are what set a wife and husband's relationship apart from all their others. They can visit, eat with, give a greeting hug and kiss to friends and other family members. Being intimate and having a sexual relationship is what makes theirs a special relationship.

If God intended pleasure and a sense of loving commitment to be part of the basis for initiating sexual togetherness, then couples may be missing something He wants them to have if they give up all sexual experiences—love play and intercourse. If they can keep their attentions vital and satisfying without intercourse, their choice could work for them.

Can senior citizens really enjoy sex as much as young couples?

Yes, they can. In fact, some have told me that they enjoy sex more now than they ever did before. Here are some of the reasons they give. They have more time and are more relaxed. They don't have to rush through their days, worry about getting enough sleep, or try to fit sex into an impossibly busy schedule. They have privacy and don't have to worry about anyone hearing them—they can talk right out loud! They have the luxury of being able to make love any time during the day. Sometimes the morning hours are especially good for firmer erections. They feel freer to talk about what is pleasurable to them in lovemaking, and if they are aging gratefully and gracefully, they are no longer as concerned about the body-aging changes as they were in their forties and fifties. We could add here that they have learned through the years that there is more to sexuality than intercourse and practice all the loving attentions that can mean so much to both wives and husbands. They might even say, "Eat your hearts out, newlyweds!"

General Questions

Is it advisable to marry after eighty or eighty-five?

Marriage at any age deserves a lot of thought, so I am pleased that you are asking for help with this decision. Sometimes older people do not take enough time to think things through and rush into marriage before they have considered all the things we ask young people to think about. It may be even more important for older people. All too often they rush into second or third marriages because they are lonely, and believe that their past experience makes it possible for them to know what is best for them now. But since they probably each have their own families now who will be affected, they need to explore what this will mean socially, medically, and financially—as well as emotionally. Many unpleasant wrangles, which have sometimes caused painful family fights, could have been averted if there had been a clearer understanding of what this marriage would mean to each person involved.

Some children have a difficult time accepting their parent's remarriage. But we would hope that for the most part they would be sensitive to the needs of their parent—at any age. Having your own home with a loving spouse is a much more desirable way of living for most people than being alone or living with someone else.

Both parties to this decision should have a pretty good idea of what they each expect from one another sexually. If one has no desire to be sexually active and the other has high hopes of what this can mean, it is going to be a real problem. They must be honest with one another and be willing to make whatever adjustments the circumstances may call for.

When these cautions have been considered, I think it would be great for two such mature people to find happiness together. If each has been in a good marriage, they realize how much they can gain by having a congenial companion. We hope they have many years to enjoy together.

I have arthritis and wonder if we should just give up on having intercourse. Sometimes it is too uncomfortable.

The ills that come along to afflict the later years of our lives can bring what seem like a roadblock to sexual interludes. Let me give you a few suggestions to try before you give up!

Some arthritis victims find that they routinely feel better at certain times of the day. Monitor yourself to see if that is your case and choose that time. If you take some type of medicine every few hours to keep you comfortable, make sure one of those dosages is a half hour or so before you plan for your love-in. If heat helps your aches, apply the heating pad or whatever you use to the aching parts just prior to lovemaking, so that you will be most relaxed and comfortable. Then have lots of pillows of several sizes around so that you can tuck them under parts of your body that need to be bolstered and kept from strain.

Putting all these together may at first seem burdensome, but it will soon become quite routine and should assure some time of easy movement. Some people have reported that having sex gives them a more relaxed feeling as one of its benefits. It also builds up their good feelings about themselves. Both of these are worth the planning it takes. So don't give up easily!

NO RETIREMENT AGE FOR SEXUALITY

God gave me the most wonderful man a woman ever had, and we have been married ___ years [a nice high number!]. Boy, do I love my man!

I think you can understand why I kept this question for the last in this chapter! What a wonderful testimony to a loving relationship—sexual and otherwise—between two aging lovers. I am sure there are many other couples who feel just as delighted with one another. May the reading of these last pages hearten some who might not feel quite so enthusiastic. May they be encouraged, now, to make their love offering for one another altogether splendid.

The conclusion of the whole matter . . .

Can we reach some conclusion following our discussion of the many aspects of sexuality? I believe that we can, and once again we are going to ask Solomon to guide us. He was inspired to present two important concepts. The first is that sexuality, as in God's plan, brings great pleasure. When it has God's love for its model, it will include continuity, fidelity, involvement, validation, gentleness, strength, and delight. Furthermore, God reminds us of this love He has for us over and over again. He doesn't mind saying "I love you" in many ways, many times. Part of the reason is probably that He recognizes our need to be reminded often. But I think something else is involved. I believe He enjoys telling us He loves us. His love is so great that it just overflows in words.

Solomon reminds us that this love involving a wife and husband has a joyous component, a sensuous aspect appealing to and involving all the senses. That summarizes the first concept.

Arriving at the second concept did not come easily for Solomon. For many years he disregarded God's will in many areas of his life, including the sexual. When he forgot God, he was involved in "madness and folly" (Ecclesiastes 1:17). He records, "I denied myself nothing my eyes desired; I refused my heart no pleasure" (Ecclesiastes 2:10, NIV). But after these excesses, he had to admit that this lifestyle was not bringing him happiness; in fact, just the opposite. He eventually found no pleasure in them. Emptiness, meaninglessness, restlessness, and hopelessness were the results he experienced. I have always appreciated Solomon's forthright confession. It has helped many a jaded person to recognize the folly of that road.

THE CONCLUSION OF THE WHOLE MATTER . . .

But Solomon makes an amazing turnaround, after a very careful and thorough self-study. He spared nothing in confronting himself. Then he says, with conviction, "Now all has been heard; here is the conclusion of the matter: Fear God and keep his commandments, for this is the whole duty of man" (Ecclesiastes 12:13).

Which commandments? Well, most certainly the one that forbids sexual immorality. But I think all Christians would agree that it would include Jesus' personal instruction to "love one another as I have loved you." Do we really comprehend all that is saying? It would comprise loving our spouses with faithfulness, eagerness, gentleness, forgiveness, consideration, demonstrations, and dialogue. What a challenge!

When we, with God's help, grow into this experience together, the sexual oneness God intended for wives and husbands will indeed be a joyous and at the same time a sanctified delight. Then we can truly affirm the words of the beloved:

> I belong to my lover,
> and his desire is for me.
> Come, my lover, let us go to the countryside,
> let us spend the night in the villages.
> Let us go early to the vineyards
> to see if the blossoms have opened,
> and if the pomegranates are in bloom—
> There I will give you my love.
>
> *Song of Solomon 7:10-12, NIV*

Read someone else's mail...
(without feeling guilty!)

Miriam Wood has received and answered letters in the *Adventist Review* for years. Now you can read the best of Miriam's mail in her new book, **Dear Miriam**.

Whether the subject is pantyhose at foot-washing, the resurrection of pets, or surrogate motherhood, you will benefit from Miriam's spiritual gifts of insight and discernment as you read her balanced and biblically based responses.

Dear Miriam is entertaining. But more than that, it is a window into the hearts and minds of real Christians who also happen to be real people with real questions . . . like yours.

US$7.95/Cdn$9.95. 128 pages. Paper.

Please photocopy and complete form below.

❏ *Dear Miriam*
   US$7.95/Cdn$9.95.

Please add applicable sales tax and 15% (US$2.50 minimum) to cover postage and handling.

Name _____
Address _____
City _____
State _____ Zip _____

Price $ _____   Order from your Adventist Book Center or ABC
Postage $ _____   Mailing Service, P.O. Box 7000, Boise, Idaho
Sales Tax $ _____   83707. Prices subject to change without notice.
TOTAL $ _____   Make check payable to Adventist Book Center.

© 1990 Pacific Press Publishing Association 2225